Ruby —

Tomorrow begins today

For your dream!

Smith

# NO FEAR OF TRYING

## HAROLD IVAN SMITH

THOMAS NELSON PUBLISHERS

Nashville

~~~~~~~~~~~

**TO SEVEN DREAMERS**

FRANCIS RICHARD SCORBEE
MICHAEL JOHN SMITH
RONALD ERWIN MCNAIR
ELLISON SHOJI ONIZUKA
JUDITH ARLENE RESNIK
GREGORY B. JARVIS
SHARON CHRISTA MCAULIFFE

*Who on January 28, 1986,
proved that "the future doesn't belong
to the faint-hearted
but to the brave."
They gave their dreams all they had.*

Published in Nashville, Tennessee, by Thomas Nelson, Inc., and distributed in Canada by Lawson Falle, Ltd., Cambridge, Ontario.

Printed in the United States of America.

Scripture quotations are from THE NEW KING JAMES VERSION of the Bible. Copyright © 1979, 1980, 1982, Thomas Nelson, Inc., Publishers.

**Library of Congress Cataloging-in-Publication Data**

Smith, Harold Ivan, 1947–
  No fear of trying.

  1. Conduct of life.  I. Title.
BJ1581.2.S57  1988     158'.1      88–22514
ISBN 0-8407-7622-5

# CONTENTS

# 1

## RESCUE YOUR DREAM
## FROM THE BASEMENT

Can you imagine living in a basement for your entire life? I can't. Yet this is what can happen to dreamers who let their dreams go astray.

Dr. Haller Nutt's family lived in a basement for more than a century: 111 years to be exact. In fact, their basement and the uncompleted superstructure above it are now a museum in Natchez, Mississippi, called Longwood.

Dr. Nutt, a physician-cotton planter, dreamed of a new home. Wealthy enough to have whatever he wanted, Nutt dreamed of a plantation that would "set the style" for future southern mansions. He had a site. He had a name— Longwood. So he searched for an architect who could convert his dream from some rough sketches into blueprints and finally into reality. Samuel Sloan of Philadelphia seemed to be the man.

Haller Nutt bubbled with excitement as he approved Sloan's final bold design: an octagon-shaped mansion, with eight rooms on each of the six floors, grouped around a six-story rotunda and capped with a sixteen-sided Byzantine onion-shaped dome. The South had never seen anything like it.

Nutt's dream found its way to England, France, and Italy, to craftsmen who created elaborate wood furnishings, marble mantles, statues and stairways, and splendid tapestries. He spared no expense: always the best.

Simultaneously in the South, another dream was unfolding; some would eventually label it a "nightmare." People talked of secession, perhaps war. Nutt, a northern sympathizer, dismissed the talk as the agitation of hotheads. Longwood totally dominated his thinking: The house must be built, the gardens completed, and then, a round of balls held to show it off to the elite of southern society.

Northern carpenters began construction of Nutt's eight-sided "castle" in 1860 and by mid-1861 had completed the outside of the building. The massive dome sparkled in the sunshine. But the carpenters' work plans suddenly changed.

Abruptly, the men dropped their hammers and saws and headed north to join the Union Army. Once and for all, they would put an end to the menace of slavery, which they had seen firsthand and which gave men like Nutt the wealth to build such houses. "What about my house?" Haller demanded.

"More important things to do," the workers answered.

Haller thought the war would, at most, delay the completion of his dream home six months. When the war continued, he moved his family into the basement "for the time being." But the Civil War slowly began to destroy his wealth and his dream. Union soldiers burned or confiscated a million-dollars worth of prime cotton and land. The materials to complete Nutt's house were needed in the war effort and even if they had been available, Nutt had no money to buy them.

In 1864, his dream shattered, Haller Nutt died. The next generation would have to complete his dream. But sadly, the house became the dream-legacy for another generation, then another. Finally, after Haller's descendants had lived in the basement for 111 years, the family deeded Longwood to the Pilgrimage Garden Club. It was designated a national historic landmark, open daily to the public: an unfinished monument to a lost dream.[1]

I visited Longwood one day and came away with my mind whirling. How many people had I met, listened to, counseled with, who lived in the basement of their dreams? How many had once had dreams as ornate as Haller Nutt's? How many had been scoffed at by neighbors? How many had pursued and been broken by their dreams, mangled by circumstances beyond their control?

As I drove away from the mansion site that beautiful fall afternoon, I reviewed some of my dreams. Could I, too, like Haller Nutt and his descendants, be living in the basement of an uncompleted dream? Are you? What has happened to your dreams, to your "I want to . . ."? Have they become past tense: "I *wanted* to . . ."? Have you forgotten some of those once cherished and nurtured dreams?

## DREAMS COME TO ALL PEOPLE

Each one of us has spent some time dreaming, lying by the seashore or in a grassy woods, wondering "What if . . ." All of us, when we were young, often boasted, "When I get big, I'm gonna . . ." and we filled in the blank. One day's declaration might be 180 degrees, even 360 degrees, different from the previous day's. Many of our dreams began with a childhood boast and were completed in ways even more fantastic than the dreams themselves.

I love to read the nametags of people who enroll in my seminars (perhaps because my name is so common). Whenever I find a unique name, I ask questions about it, for somewhere behind that name is a story—a dreamer's story. Perhaps a grandfather or a grandmother was an immigrant, who began that long journey, leaving the familiar in order to embrace the unknown. Some of my participants are now one, two, or even three generations from the old country; they cannot fathom what their ancestors faced and felt. No doubt their foreparents would gasp, "I never dreamed . . ." at the success and achievements of their progeny.

Imagine an Italian couple, arriving in New York City with nothing but their hopes. Did they have a smidgen of a dream that sixty years later the governor of New York would be their son, Mario Cuomo?[2]

Did that Swiss widow, with two small children, who came to America because of her fear that the Germans would invade her homeland, ever dream that thirty-five years later her daughter, Madeline Kunin, would be the governor of Vermont?[3]

Dreams do not respect skin color.

Dreams do not respect gender.

Dreams do not observe neighborhood boundaries.

Dreams do not require that you have to walk, talk, see, or hear.

Dreams are not limited by age.

Dreams come to everyone.

One of the saddest questions in our world is, "Whatever happened to that dream of mine to . . .?" Has someone's criticism driven your dream into the basement?

Some people have been so bruised by previous attempts to fulfill their dream that they withdraw into protective shells and "mothball" their dreams.

*The Atlanta Constitution* ran a fascinating article about the process of mothballing battleships like the *Iowa,* and the *New Jersey,* and the *Wisconsin,* which were built during World War II. These ships, weighing 58,000 tons, with seventeen inches of armor and superior speed, helped America win that war.

In an era of the modern navy, the ships were deemed outdated and were drydocked. As the boilers cooled, the network of hundreds of miles of pipes were drained. Fuel and all flammable liquids were siphoned out. Motors were cleaned thoroughly; pumps were filled with preservative chemicals.

All openings were covered with sealants or metal hatches to prevent moisture from entering. Winches, machinery, and any moving parts were covered in airtight igloos. Dehumidifiers were installed throughout the ships. Some critics fumed that it would have been cheaper to have sunk them.

For twenty-five years these mothballed relics were monitored by the U.S. Navy's Ship Maintenance Facility staff, specialists in the art of preserving ships.

Then the Reagan administration called for an immediate increase in the size of the Navy, and the ships were recommissioned. When senior staff boarded the *Iowa,* they said it was as if the ship's crew had merely gone on weekend leave. Duty schedules, posted twenty-five years earlier, had not even yellowed in the dark, cool air.[4]

I suspect that's also true of our dreams. How about recommissioning your mothballed, well-preserved dreams, which are still untested, even though years have passed since inception?

### Intersections

I suggest that we come to "intersections" in our lives: places in the heart where courage conquers fear, where compassion bests cowardice and shame. In such moments, we are never as alone as we assume. Deep within our spirit, an urge stirs us to shake off our limitations, our cultural intimidations—"What will people say/think?"—to step forward and to do the right thing.

Some label such moments coincidence or chance. Indeed, one could reasonably argue that in most of these "opportunities" there is little, if anything, to indicate that a decision or choice is to be precedent shattering. Whatever you call it, the person who seizes such opportunities is the one who eventually becomes known for his or her dream.

What dreamer, even as you read this, is close—dangerously close—to abandoning the dream? What discouraged dreamer wonders today, *Will I make any difference?*

### YOUR DREAM CAN MAKE A DIFFERENCE

Dreams are all about us. Almost every facet of our lives is influenced by someone's dreams. In fact, it is amazing what one dream can do to change a way of life. As I write today, it is a cold afternoon in Seattle. There is, however, enough daylight so I don't have to turn on the lights. However, in another hour my writing will be over for the day unless I use Mr. Edison's invention, electric lights. My great-grandfather's workday was controlled by daylight; now we have more "day" to accomplish work.

As soon as this draft is completed, I'll proof it using a Bic pen, another dream product. Hoping to supplement his meager schoolteacher's salary, George Stafford Parker developed the inexpensive disposable pen to sell to his pupils. His concept was later refined by a clever young Frenchman, Marcel Bich, whose "Bic" pens would become famous around the world.[5]

Next, I'll type another draft of the chapter on a word processor *(what a dream)* and eventually mail the final draft to the publisher via another dream: express mail (some authors send final drafts through a telephone modem).

Other people's dreams have affected my life as an author.

Your dream may not give the world tomorrow's VCR-like technological advance. Still, your dream could be as important. Every so often, the world needs a break—a hula hoop, a frisbee, a Rubik's Cube. The smiles, the giggles from such inventions make us a little more humane and help us take ourselves and our problems a little less seriously.

Your dream may not be a thing but an idea. Sometimes the world needs its lens polished so that it has a fresh look at the needs of its citizenry, from the wealthiest to the poorest. That may be your dream, your opportunity, your invitation to make a difference. For example, during the famine in Africa millions of people were hungry and homeless, exposed to the cold nights. There weren't enough blankets for everyone. Some, particularly children, got pneumonia and died.

A British engineer in Ethiopia, Roy Higgins had spent a lot of time thinking about the problems he saw daily in his work with World Vision. One day, while relaxing, he absent-mindedly played with the bubble-plastic wrapping from a newly arrived radio. As he wrapped the plastic around his hand, his hand felt warm. *Eureka,* he thought.

Higgins immediately ordered more of the bubble-pack material and, under the supervision of Dr. Hector Jalipa, organized an experiment. He cut out one hundred sleeping bags from the bolt of plastic, recognizing several benefits. The plastic was lightweight, insulative for warmth, protective from the rain; and because of the bubbles, people would not risk suffocation as with other plastics.

Initially, people were skeptical and rejected the idea as weird. But the bubble-plastic sleeping bags worked and saved lives.

World Vision soon ordered 5,000 yards of bubble-plastic. The inventor of the plastic had designed it for packing and shipping; a compassionate man found an application the inventor never dreamed of.[6]

And that's not the end of the story. Now American hospitals are saying if it worked in Africa, it will work in America. So they are adapting the material for use in keeping premature babies warm.[7] Ideas spin off unpredictable consequences.

Some of the consequences may be unpleasant. In the last few years entrepreneurs and small businesses have generated great ideas, which are then stolen by giant corporations. Francis Goldwyn, president of Manhattan Toy Co., Ltd., said, "When you design a product that flies off the shelves, it's just a matter of time before someone copies it."[8]

Greeting cards are big business in this country. You've probably received a Hallmark card or a Blue Mountain Arts card on some occasion. Blue Mountain Arts cards feature the poetry of Susan Polis Schutz, whose words have struck responsive chords within thousands of people. Her distinctive greeting cards are hot products for greeting card stores.

Hallmark had long been an innovative corporation. First, they introduced the concept of the greeting card—simply a decorative postcard. Then they developed the card-in-an-envelope so popular today. However, Hallmark had missed the younger generation, who didn't want to buy the same cards their parents (and grandparents) bought.

Schutz, who owns Blue Mountain, turned down Hallmark's offer to buy her out. And though she was flattered, she thought that was the end of the story. Wrong.

In April 1986, as Susan was browsing in a California card shop, she was surprised to find only three of her cards on sale. She was even more shocked when she discovered they weren't her cards at all: They were Hallmark copies. "When you held the two cards together, you couldn't tell them apart," she said. If she could mistake them, so would consumers.

When Susan contacted the giant cardmaker, they informed her that Hallmark didn't copy cards. Susan and her husband had copyrighted their poems and artwork, but Hallmark had gone one step further and had copycatted the look.

Blue Mountain Arts hired an attorney who specialized in "trade dress," or intellectual and creative property, and filed a fifty-million-dollar suit against Hallmark. In November 1986, a judge slapped an injunction on Hallmark ordering them to stop marketing eighty-three cards that resembled the work of Susan Polis Schutz.

Hallmark complied with the court order.

Soon there were eighty-three new look-alike cards on the Hallmark racks. And Hallmark lawyers are appealing. Susan Polis Schutz and tiny (by comparison) Blue Mountain Arts have won the first round of a legal battle.[9]

That's why you need to keep careful records of your dream. Sure, someone could have told Susan Polis Schutz that her cards were "nice," but who would have dreamed that this lady would have ended up a major influencer of greeting card tastes? It began with a dream.

That's why at the end of each chapter in this book you will find questions which will help you put your dream into words and which could become proof of the originality of your idea, protecting your dream from being stolen or "borrowed."

Now is the time to protect your dream, even before the first hint of success.

## DREAMS SPIN OFF BOTH PREDICTABLE AND UNPREDICTABLE CONSEQUENCES

Often a dreamer begins to create with one dream in mind, but another product evolves during the process. Be alert to the value of spin-off dreams and ideas.

The same afternoon I visited Longwood, I toured another mansion in Natchez: Stanton Hall. On each end of the drawing room (a mere seventy-two feet) are wall-to-ceiling gilded mirrors, designed to catch the light from the room's massive brass chandeliers. The tour host pointed out that if you stared into one of the mirrors, you could not count the number of chandeliers reflected. Why? The two mirrors reflected each other so that you could almost see to infinity.[10]

So with the dreamer. No one can count the spin-off dreams that result from a dreamer's courage. Who would have thought that two Japanese men in 1946, Akio Morita and Masaru Ibuka, in a tiny company called Tokyo Telecommunications Engineering Company (worth less than $500) located in bombed-out Tokyo, could have set in motion the technological breakthroughs that eventually made VCRs and Walkmans commonplace in American society? If I had interviewed then those young dreamers—who were feeding themselves and their families with income from the production of replacement parts for phonographs—would you have believed me if I had argued that they had a bright future? In 1946, Ibuka wanted to make tape recorders, not VCRs or Walkmans. However, almost no one wanted to buy tape recorders. Either the public didn't know what tape recorders were (other than legal stenographers in courtrooms) or they couldn't understand what to do with them. Any editor who received my article on Tokyo Tele-communications would have growled, "They're nuts," and rejected my article.[11]

But the two Japanese men modified their dream from tape recorders to Walkmans and VCRs. As a result, the world has the Sony Corporation, an electronics pacesetter.

Or what about the crewmen of the commercial vessel who found a group of Vietnamese huddled in a small boat, floating in the Subic Bay near the Philippines in 1975? Would any of those crewmen have believed that a decade later nine-year-old Hoang Nhu Tran would graduate number one in his class from the U.S. Air Force Academy and be chosen a Rhodes Scholar, selected for three years of study at Oxford? His parents sought their dream of freedom, which led to the spin-off dream of their son's accomplishments.[12]

Like an Akio Morita, Roy Higgins, Hoang Nhu Trun, a dreamer often persists alone in his or her creative cocoon. Waiting. Watching. Wondering. Wishing.

## DARE TO DREAM

These days it takes courage to dream. Mediocrity is a lifestyle, a way of life for too many. "Take it easy" or "What's the big hurry?" or "Where's the fire?" are common expressions from laid-back people. While walking through the renovated Union Station in St. Louis, I found this calligraphy, which now hangs in my bathroom so that I can see it the first thing every morning:

> All my friends say,
> "Hey, take it easy. Where's the fire?"
> The fire, I tell them, is right here.
> And it's burning brighter than ever.
> I've always been a dreamer.
> But now I'm making
> Those dreams come true.
> World, catch me if you can.

Apparently that wisdom came from the prolific writer, Anonymous.

This book will encourage you to unpack and replant some dreamseeds, once stored in the fertile soil of your childhood imagination, now hidden in some dark basement of your spirit. It just may well be that your dream, your invention, your technological advance, has never before been more appropriate or needed than now, *"for such a time as this."*[13]

Maybe your dreamseed is small, very small, about the size of a fist. Be thankful for that. This book is like a pair of binoculars to scan the horizon, to bring some distant sites or shores into perspective, into range. You will find something to help you nourish your dream.

As you read, I will ask you to wonder, to doubt, to apply the stories of dreamers to your own life.

As you read, I will ask you to evacuate your cozy comfort zones, your "I'd like to but's" that keep your dream in the basement, like Haller Nutt's.

I will ask you to discard your "if only's"—memories or excuses that keep your binoculars pointed toward yesterday instead of tomorrow.

I will ask you to take some baby steps today—within the next twenty-four-hours—toward unveiling your dream.

And I will be doing the same thing because I, too, fight the temptation to focus my binoculars on yesterday. And I too have "if only's." In fact, by this point in your reading, you may be wondering about my qualifications and credibility. You may have looked at the book jacket and my picture and the brief biographical sketch. But that doesn't tell you enough about my dreams and dream style.

Why should you read me rather than the other authors who have written on this or similar themes? Why didn't the publisher contract with a "name" to do this book? Because I am a fellow pilgrim *with you*—one who is still working at the dream instead of coasting. Together we will investigate the process of turning our dreams into reality.

Let me draw back the curtains on my dream. I have wanted to write for as long as I can remember, a desire that was profoundly influenced by an English teacher. You probably expect me to say that he early recognized my writing talents and encouraged me. Hardly. In front of the class, he snarled, "Smith, you will never amount to anything. You are a loser." His remarks produced a clamor of laughter from my pals.

I spent twenty years trying to disprove his assessment. When I completed my doctorate and my first novel, *Priscilla and Aquila,* was published, I mailed him an autographed copy with this note: "I'm not sure why you said what you said, but that day in senior English class has had an incredible wallop on my life. I've tried to prove you wrong and I have."

I was disappointed when he didn't write back.

Even though I've now written more than a dozen books and more than a hundred magazine articles, I have felt like a second-string writer. I have walked into bookstores and discovered they didn't have a single copy of any of my books. I didn't have name recognition.

Somehow, I decided that my dream would be to write a best seller. Then I would be somebody. Or would I? What about my ministry called Tear-Catchers, which encourages sympathetic suffering, works for the interests of single adults, and researches emerging issues of social concern for the religious community? What about my new company, Harold Ivan Smith and Associates, which researches the single adult in the workplace and consults with corporations and the military on related issues?

In the process of writing this book, I have learned that my dream is not to write a best seller or to be a celebrity writer. My dream is to write books and articles that make a difference. Then my words and ideas will help people, such as yourself, in a busy, hectic world to explore, embrace, and pursue their dreams.

My dream is that by choices and commitments, my gravestone will read, "He made a difference."

I don't want to be your hero or guru. But I do want to be your cheerleader, even for those of you living in the fourth quarter of life. There is always time to add another chapter to your story.

A dream is a journey not a destination. And the road to dreams is wide enough that we can go together so that if I stumble, you can help me. And if you stumble, I can help you.

What about your dream? Isn't it worth liberating from the basement? Doesn't the world deserve to have a better look at your dream? Isn't it possible that your dream would encourage others to dream?

All of us have known too many people who are living in the basement. All of us know too many people who whine, "You can't get there from *here*."

This book is a great place to launch a dream. Go back to the Table of Contents. You probably skipped over it or skimmed it lightly. It is more than a list of chapter titles. It is the stairway out of the basement. It is the roadmap for getting from your here to the there of your dream.

Bringing your dream to life will be the biggest challenge you'll ever face. It's not impossible even in an improbable world, if you follow the ten steps outlined in this book.

After you finish this first chapter, I suggest that you sift through the ideas you've stored in the attic or basement of your mind. Which ones deserve to be resurrected? Write them in a journal and refer to them in the next chapter as we evaluate your dreams.

You can open some books to any page, begin to read, and find some good things. I would ask that you stay with me, chapter by chapter. Why? Because each chapter will give you practical hints on taking the next step, making the right decision. Each chapter builds on the previous chapter to form a network of decisions that will put your dream into action. This book is a roadmap to your dream destination.

My visit to historic Longwood jarred me. A century and a decade of living in a mansion's basement. However elegant, a basement is still a basement. For more than one hundred years an uncompleted mansion stood over the Nutt's elegant basement.

If you are living in the basement of a dream, *No Fear of Trying* will help you to resume the construction of *your* dream.

You are the only person in the world with the strength to have your dream and then to make it happen.

A lifetime is not too long to cling to a dream. But a lifetime is too long to cling to a dreamseed.

Give your dream a chance.

I dare you.

~~~~~~~~~~~~~~~~~~~~~~~~~~~~~~

At the end of each chapter, you will find questions to help you discover your dreams and choose the path to pursue them. You may want to record your thoughts in a diary or journal.

When I was young I often boasted, "When I get big, I'm gonna _____," or more recently, "Someday, when I get time, I'm going to _____."

All of us have made such statements before. Take time to write out the dreams of your youth.

Now write out the dreams of your adulthood.

# 2

## STEP ONE

# EVALUATE YOUR DREAM

How much does a dream cost? Can you afford a dream? Often it costs more, at least in terms of self-respect, not to complete a dream. That's another reason to make sure your dream has your initials on it.

Jesus spoke to that question. "For which of you, intending to build a tower, does not sit down first and count the cost, whether he has enough to finish it—lest, after he has laid the foundation, and is not able to finish it, all who see it begin to mock him."[1]

Most dreams are achieved because a dreamer counted the cost. Credentials, money, resources are important, but the dreamer has to evaluate the costs for meaning. For example, in the early days of the airplane, who would have foreseen the plane being used as a weapon.

Meredith Tax, in his book *Rivington Street,* described the tension between a father and a son in the 1910s because of the son's love for the airplane.

> Denzell tried to convince his father that this hobby was of potential use. Someday airplanes would be used for transportation, mail, hunting, racing; they might even be adapted by the military in the unlikely event of another war. But his father was adamant. . . . "It's too dangerous. As long as your money is in my control, you'll have to stay out of those things."[2]

Imagine predicting, in 1910, that someday there would be planes capable of carrying 400 passengers and tons of cargo, flying to Europe from New York in a few hours.

Did Lindbergh understand the potential consequences when he flew that tiny *Spirit of Saint Louis* across the Atlantic? Could he foresee a day, not two decades ahead, when a plane called the *Enola Gay* would fly over two Japanese cities and drop atomic bombs that forever changed the history of mankind by ushering in the atomic age? I doubt it.

Dreams are unlikely to become reality without continuous evaluation.

Let's examine some of the questions you should be asking.

## WHEN DID MY DREAM BEGIN?

Do you know when your dream began? Some dreamseeds are first planted in pain. Martin Luther King's dream didn't begin two weeks before his historic speech on the steps of the Lincoln Memorial on August 24, 1963. His dream began in his childhood, when he first realized that some hated him because of the color of his skin.

Some physicians and nurses admit their dream began as a result of being cared for as a child by a kind doctor or nurse.

My dream to write began in a fifth grade classroom at Henry B. Schnafner Elementary School in Louisville, Kentucky. Mrs. Christine Regan, my fifth grade teacher, assigned each of her students to write a poem on the theme of brotherhood. The next day she asked for volunteers to share their poems.

I stood and read. The next thing I knew she had crossed the room and pulled the poem from my hand.

"Oh, class, I have goose bumps," she shrieked (she really shrieked). "Read it again. Class, listen to this."

Minutes later, I found myself reading the poem to our principal, Mr. Gene Shrader. Eventually, I read the composition at the monthly PTA meeting.

A few simple words started a dream within me. I liked the

way people responded to my words. Goose bumps, huh? Well, needless to say, not everyone since then has been so complimentary of my writing.

Ralph Baker's dream began one night in 1980 as he watched scenes of the tragic MGM fire in Las Vegas that took eighty-four lives and injured hundreds. Most of the victims were trapped on the upper floors of the twenty-six-story hotel, beyond the reach of fire-department ladders and nets.

Baker, a third-generation truck driver, realized what happened in Las Vegas could have happened in any one of the thousand high-rise hotels in America. As he drove his truck, he toyed with solutions. "A lot of people wait for bad things to happen, then try to figure out what to do. Not me. When I see a problem in the making, I try to head it off before it can occur." But what would Baker, a trucker, know about high-rise fires?

His dream: *life chutes,* a circular netting that could be attached to the side of the building. Then, a person could simply climb out of the window or rooftop, feet first, and step into the chute. Gravity would take care of the rest.

Baker started with a five-story building. Then, in 1984, he recruited several volunteers, including his daughter, twenty-five, and grandson, four, to evacuate a sixteen-story dorm at the University of Delaware. "It turned out to be just like going down a giant slide," said one volunteer. To up the ante, Wayne Carter, a thirty-six-year-old paraplegic, took the plunge too.

Two fire departments have purchased models of the life chute; more will follow. Baker's hope for his dream product: "To one day turn on a newscast and see people sliding down my chute . . . saved from dying in a fire."[3]

Baker knows when his dream began.

When did *your* dream begin?

Some of us can recognize the start. We can name a day, a time, or a place. For others, it is all rather vague. But, at some point the dream began, and it's important to know when so that we have a time line to measure our progress.

## CAN ANYONE ELSE ACHIEVE MY DREAM?

There is no shortage of copycat dreamers. Let an entrepreneur or a company put a new product on the market, imitators will soon be on their heels. An article in the *Seattle Times* on the development of Japanese electronic pianos captured my attention. "Our goal is to produce a fine piano rivaling a Steinway," said Kenji Murakani, press agent for Yamaha. A noble ambition, I conceded. I was not as impressed, however, with the attitude of Teruo Hiyoshi, who directs the making of all musical instruments for Yamaha. "If someone succeeds, we can very quickly catch up."

"How can you catch up to someone's piano?" the interviewer asked.

"We can copy."

On the other hand, some people have, in the midst of an experience, realized the dream was not theirs to achieve.[4] Still they have received satisfaction from contributing to a dream.

Dr. William Greathouse was president of a small Bible college in Tennessee. A theologian-scholar, he dreamed of the school's potential as an accredited liberal arts college. He worked tirelessly to shape his dream and to share that potential. He raised millions of dollars, built buildings, attracted faculty, and developed boosters. Yet the dream was not realized during his presidency. Dr. Greathouse shared the victory *at a distance,* as president of another institution. He laid much of the groundwork, yet another reaped the applause.

My work as the first general director of a single adult ministry for a denomination was an incredible uphill challenge. When I was appointed, I weighed the decision to give up my academic post in California. I vacillated. I loved California, my college, my colleagues, yet I also appreciated the opportunity of the new position.

Everyone recognized the need to launch a national program to reach divorced people, widowed men and women, and single parents. After all, I had authored the study that documented the need. To complicate the decision, I was in love and wanted to complete my doctorate. To move 1,500 miles east at that time was tempting, but so was staying put to complete other dreams.

I shared my struggle with the college chaplain, Reuben Welch. "A lot of people can be director of admissions at Point Loma College," Reuben said, "but not everyone can be general director of single adult ministries. I'd go!"

It was *my* dream. I resigned my academic post at midyear, said my good-bys, and moved to Kansas City. For nine years I have watched the dream unfold, far beyond any of my expectations or hopes.

What about your dream? Can anyone else achieve *your* dream? If not, it's worth your full-time commitment.

### IS MY DREAM NOBLE?

I would paraphrase Paul's words, "Whatever things are noble, whatever things are just, whatever things are pure, whatever things are lovely, whatever things are of good report, if there is any virtue and if there is anything praiseworthy—*dream* on these things."[5]

I think of the Grimké sisters, who lived a life of ease and comfort in the antebellum South as daughters of one of South Carolina's wealthiest and more politically powerful men, State Supreme Court Justice John F. Grimké. They probably sat on the porch of their plantation house, sipping cool lemonade. Servants were at their elbows, anticipating any need Sarah and Angelina might have.

Normal dreams for girls like the Grimkés probably went something like this: "When I grow up, I want to meet a beau (with money), perhaps tall, dark, and handsome, who will build me a plantation house, bigger and more grandiose than any other." In the magnolia-scented air, such dreams seemed natural.

But Sarah Grimké had a noble dream: to see a day when slavery would be abolished. She didn't wait until she grew up. Instead, Sarah defied the law and taught her personal slaves to read. (Her father had drafted the law making this illegal!) Eventually she and her sister decided to free their slaves, a decision that infuriated their neighbors and, especially, the fellow members of the Third Presbyterian Church in South Charleston. Then Sarah dared to stand up in a church meeting and urge other members to do the same—this in an era when it was thought scandalous for a woman to speak in public or on political issues.[6]

The two sisters continued to speak out against slavery and were exiled to the North. "Never come back to South Carolina," they were warned. But they found audiences in the North anxious to hear them. In one twenty-three-week period, as the sisters toured New England, they spoke to 40,000 people. To have spoken to half that many would have been remarkable. On Wednesday, February 21, 1838, the Grimkés made history: Angelina became the first woman in American history ever to address a legislative body. The Massachusetts State House was packed that afternoon, not with people who came to listen but with those who came to scoff and laugh, to see a woman make a fool of herself and of her sex. The taverns near the State House emptied to give patrons a chance to get a good seat for "the show."

Angelina had to walk on the desks in order to reach the front. When she stood to speak she was greeted by hisses. Three times the chairman stopped her to try to get order in the chamber.

"I stand before you a southerner," she began, almost in a whisper, "exiled from the land of my birth by the sound of the lash and the piteous cry of the slave. I stand before you as a repentant slaveholder." Slowly her voice gained confidence and authority; the chamber quieted.

> I stand before you a moral being, and as a moral being I feel that I owe it to the suffering slave and to the deluded master, to my country and to the world, to do all that I can do to overturn a system of complicated crimes, built upon broken hearts and prostrate bodies of my countrymen in chains and cemented by the blood, sweat and tears of my sisters in bonds.[7]

The chairman, who stood near Angelina, fought tears. That afternoon, Angelina Grimké ushered in a new era, not just in the fight against slavery, but in the fight for the rights of women in American society.

The attack upon her was bitter, personal, vindictive. She and her sister were labeled "abnormal creatures lusting for attention," old maids anxious to attract men, cranks. But they didn't give up under fire. They wrote *American Slavery As It Really Is* in 1839, which soon sold more copies than any other book on slavery; 100,000 copies sold the first year. That book heavily influenced Harriet Beecher Stowe's draft of *Uncle Tom's Cabin*.[8]

Two courageous dreamers stepped into the void and offered their brains and their voices to end slavery.

Take another look at Paul's list: *true; noble; just; pure; lovely; of good report*. Can you use such terms for your dream?

Commit yourself to a noble dream. Be willing, in the words of the song, "to march into hell for a heavenly cause."

## WHO NOURISHES MY DREAM?

Parents? Friends? Teachers? Colleagues? Other dreamers? Anyone?

All of us need cheerleaders, though, in reality, we may have to settle for *one* cheerleader or a part-time one. I was the first in my family to attend college, let alone to go on to graduate school. At each of my graduations, Dad scratched his head and asked (almost fearing the answer), "What's next?" Because I was the first, it was difficult for my family to nourish my dream. Later, the idea of being a writer, of sitting at a typewriter for hours and hours, seemed outrageous to my father, who had worked forty years for the same company. What about fringe benefits? What about the security of a regular paycheck every two weeks?

For a long time I envied the affirmation systems of some of my friends, until I met John Moore, a college professor who lavishly heaped praise and encouragement on *all* of his students. He stretched our dreams; he daily cleaned the lenses of the binoculars aimed at our dreams.

A dream needs support. A dreamer needs encouragement to counteract the criticism of the conspicuous silence of those who either don't know how or refuse to encourage.

That's why I am excited about the development of the mentoring concept in the business community. The idea consists of a person taking a younger colleague or associate under the wings to offer guidance and encouragement. This has been particularly beneficial for women in business because they have not easily profited from the "good ole boys'" support system. A mentor helps to keep the dream focused and sometimes offers a healthy dose of reality.

James Newton has documented well the mentor concept in his book *Uncommon Friends*, the story of his friendship (and the interlocking friendships) with five great pioneers: Henry Ford, Thomas Edison, Charles Lindbergh, Alexis Carrel, and Harvey Firestone.

Newton became friends with Thomas and Mina Edison when he built a housing development across from the Edison home in Fort Meyers, Florida. The Edisons, in turn, introduced Newton to their friends, the Henry Fords. Naturally, Newton wanted to know how Edison and Ford had become such good friends and eventually neighbors.

According to Edison's story, the Edison Illuminating Company was having its annual convention at Manhattan Beach, outside New York City. One night at dinner, Alex Dow, the head of Detroit Edison, said to Mr. Edison, "Over there's a young fellow who's made a gas car." Immediately Edison was interested because he had developed the first electric car. Rather than see young Henry Ford as an upstart or competitor, Edison invited him over to his table and began to fire questions at him. Impressed with the answers, his final words to Ford were, "Keep at it!"[9]

And Ford did.

Later, Newton quizzed Ford about the origin of the friendship. Had this particular event taken place as Edison had de-scribed it?

"I should say I remember the day," Henry Ford began. "It was the turning point for me. Mr. Edison listened to me very pa-tiently. Then he banged his fist on the table and said, 'Young man, that's the thing. Your car is self-contained—no boiler, no heavy battery, no smoke or steam. Keep at it!'

"You can imagine how excited I was—the man who knew the most about electricity in the world—my boyhood idol—telling me my gas car was better than an electric car! He was the first to give me real encouragement that my dream would work! Well, that boyhood idol became my manhood friend."[10]

When that encouragement paid rich dividends, Ford gave Edison the first car off each Ford Assembly line: the first Model T, the first Model A, the first V–8, the first Lincoln. Not bad compensation for the three words *Keep at it!*

Newton wrote, "Ford never stopped thinking of ways to help Edison. He kept buying the newest hearing aids for Edison who was all but deaf; gifts Edison routinely rejected." If he wore a hearing aid, Edison explained, "'I'd have to listen to what folks were saying and would have less time for my reading.'" Secondly, "'Mina [his wife] would make me go to church.'" Be-sides, deafness had benefits he did not want to miss out on: During his courtship with Mina, it gave him an excuse to sit much closer to her.[11]

One has to wonder if Edison had reserved his interest or lim-ited his encouragement or been too busy with the main entree that evening to have talked to young Ford, would there ever have been a Ford Motor Company. Let me bring it closer to home by sharing a personal experience.

I came from a religious background that had little apprecia-tion for the arts: films, drama, opera, and especially dance. Oh, we appreciated the arts if there were direct, obvious spiri-tual impacts. My childhood friend, George, became fascinated with puppets after we saw an evangelist-ventriloquist at youth camp. Many church folk encouraged George to explore ventriloquism. "What a blessing you could be," the older members told him, although still somewhat skeptical.

But the first encouragement stirred George's curiosity, which soon spilled over into other areas. George pursued drama, then dance. The same people who had given the initial encouragement suddenly disapproved. George had stepped over some mystical line. A weaker individual than George would have caved in and abandoned his or her dream to go to New York City and beyond. But George, well, he dug in. He knew a dream's monogram when he saw it.

In our years in the National Forensic League and Thespians at Butler High in Louisville, Kentucky, we participated together in a lot of speech tournaments and plays. I was as active and enthusiastic about oratory and extemporaneous speaking as he was about drama and dance, but I justified my interest and talent because I was going into "The Ministry."

Eventually we parted ways, our friendship severed. George went to Broadway and I went to a small southern college.

I could not appreciate his dream, so I would not affirm him. Nor did he affirm me. I don't know if my rejection influenced him. I arrogantly assumed my dream gift was more worthy than his. Over the years I have changed my opinion of George and the acting profession and am fascinated by ballet. George died before I could apologize.

Maybe some dreams are less worthy, even unworthy. But we can discourage the particular dream without demolishing the integrity and self-esteem of the dreamer. We must find a way to reject a particular dream without damaging the next dream as well.

Everyone has dreams that need to be appreciated and applauded. Who couldn't use more cheerleaders?

Is your dream being nourished? By whom?

## WHO HAS ATTEMPTED MY DREAM?

A dreamer has to be aware of the past: Has anyone attempted this dream before? Who? A history of the U.S. Patent Office would make fascinating reading. Alexander Graham Bell, for example, wasn't the only American inventor to tinker with the telephone. In fact, he only beat Elisha Gray to the patent office by about twenty-four hours. Had Gray moved a little faster, we might make out our phone checks today to Southwest *Gray* instead of Southwest Bell.[12]

Sometimes our dream is to supplement the dreams of others. Although Bell gets credit for inventing the telephone, its signal was too weak to make it practical. It was up to Thomas Alva Edison to develop the carbon transmitter to make the telephone commercially valuable.[13]

When Ford purchased Edison's labs, he also bought the garbage bins. He wanted to know what Edison had attempted as well as what he had achieved. Often we think of the big name historically linked to an achievement or breakthrough. We fail to honor those nameless or in-the-background colleagues who also contributed to the development.

Many dreamers have made deliberate studies of the biographies of pathfinders and trailblazers, looking for some ingredient of success or achievement to follow, some failure to avoid. History provides clues that may lead to your dream or to its achievement. That's why I try to read at least twenty biographies each year, for clues.

The goal that has long tempted mankind, that has left hundreds of dreamers frustrated, may wait for you. As President Reagan promised the nation, after the *Challenger* explosion, "There will be more shuttle flights and more shuttle crews, and yes, more volunteers, more civilians, more teachers in space. Nothing ends here. Our hopes and journeys continue."[14]

Who has attempted *your* dream?

## WILL MY DREAM HAVE A NEGATIVE IMPACT ON THOSE I LOVE?

Our society is well supplied with workaholics whose creed is no price, no sacrifice "too great." How many wheeler-dealers and movers-shakers have worked night and day to make it? How many have told themselves repeatedly, "I'm doing it for them" (wife/husband/children), only to discover that their "them" have gone elsewhere for love and affection—they couldn't wait? Jesus asked, "What will a man give in exchange for his soul?" Slightly paraphrased, that could be an equally important question: *What shall a man give in exchange for his own dream?*[15]

Some dreams have escalating costs, some of which may be hidden, unpredictable, at the time of launch. You will come to crossroads where you have to ask, *Do I/we turn back or go on?* For every one who goes forward, two turn back. And some, when they almost have their dream in their grasp, turn back.

You may get money—the chief criterion of achievement in this culture—but burglars or con men will soon want to pay attention to you. You may get the big house and have *Home Beautiful* write you up. But next, you'll need an alarm system, maybe even gates to feel safe—if then.

You may get fame. But how long will it be before you need a bodyguard? How long before you are being hounded? Sports celebrities, TV personalities, politicians pay an enormous price when they swap their privacy like a stock or bond in the market of notoriety.

Dreams have impacts. One hundred and twenty years after the Civil War, we are still trying to overcome the consequences of slavery. We are also reaping the fringe benefits of the courage of those who opposed slavery, some of whom died before seeing the dream become reality.

## CONCLUSION

Take these eleven questions and plant them deep in your mind to review the next time you have to make a major decision about your dream. On paper, they are helpful, even interesting. But if you engrave them on the walls of your spirit, I think you will move a step closer to achieving your dreams.

1. When did my dream begin?

2. Can anyone else achieve it? If so, who?

3. Will my dream make a difference? How? To whom? Will the difference be positive or negative?

4. Is my dream noble?

5. Who nourishes my dream? Who encourages me?

6. Has anyone attempted my dream?

7. To achieve my dream, I need the following:

8. Are there resources that I will have to wait for before my dream can become reality?

9. What are the barriers to my dream?

10. What can I do about each barrier?

11. If I had to describe the impact of my dream in twenty-five words or less, it would be:

# 3

# AVOID RAINCHECKS

Rainchecks. When a store has advertised a certain item and the demand is greater than the supply, the store issues a raincheck. Someday you present the raincheck and the item is yours. That's the way some people perceive dreams.

Americans are ingenious at finding ways to postpone, avoid, or get out of doing things they don't want to do.

We're into first-person-singular or plural—"you and me, babe, against the world"—living. Taking it easy. Or in the words of one hamburger chain, "having it your way" (or no way).

Is it any wonder that people transfer that habit or preference into the world of dreams? "May I please be excused from *this* dream?" Or "If it's all the same to you, I think I'll pass on this one."

Dreams can be demanding houseguests that challenge all other commitments and relationships. And those commitments do not make it easier for individuals to ignore the voices of our culture to "eat, drink, and be merry. There's always tomorrow for the dream."

Inventors struggle for years until the scientific or chemical breakthrough, years of previous research having already gone into the project. Once in the American business community, that was acceptable. But now the company itself might be in business only a few years—or months. So we want results, meaning breakthroughs and profits, immediately, thank you.

Resistance. You'd think people would rush to embrace their dreams. Not so. Foot-dragging, excuse-making, postponing—whatever term you care to use—there is no shortage of individuals who resist the dream.

It's easy to ask: What if Harriet Beecher Stowe had resisted writing *Uncle Tom's Cabin*? What if Ralph Baker had resisted developing the life chute? What if Akio Morita had resisted his dream to make tape recorders?

It's easier to answer that question this side of the decision. But there must have been voices urging them to resist their opportunities to pass on this one.

Yet one accurate answer is that, in time, some other person would have. When Queen Esther protested Mordecai's command that she plead with the king on behalf of the Jews, Mordecai wisely warned the queen that if she remained silent at that time (meaning, If you ignore this dream . . .) "relief and deliverance would arise" . . . *from another source*. Esther would have missed her opportunity. And, Mordecai added, "who knows whether you have come to the kingdom for such a time as this?"[1]

Every dreamer must ponder deep within his or her spirit the phrase *for such a time as this*. Every dreamer must have a keen sense of the now. Some dreams are too crucial to humanity to wait for you to decide your response.

Let's look at the factors that cause us to resist our dreams.

## RESISTANCE FACTOR 1: IMPATIENCE

"Fire the coach!" is the alumni cry during a losing basketball or football season at most universities. After several years of losses, few university presidents can resist. As several newly hired coaches can attest, you cannot turn a losing program into a winning one overnight. That could prompt a whole new round of "Fire the coach! Get rid of the bum!"

You've no doubt seen the slogan or bumpersticker, You Want

It *When?* That's the way some folks are with dreams: I want it. Now!

Think of Sarah Grimké, in 1829, courageously declaring that slavery was wrong. She wasn't the first southern voice to speak out against slavery. But she didn't really expect her fellow members of the Third Presbyterian Church of South Charleston to support her dream. She knew sharing the dream would be costly. She knew that slavery would not be eliminated before the next social season in Charleston. But she also knew the protest could not wait.

How many southerners bragged that the war would be over within ninety days? And how many Americans, a century later, believed that the nightmare in Vietnam would be brief? That somehow the next escalation of troops would be sufficient?

It takes days, weeks, years, perhaps decades, of consistency and effort before a "Eureka!" moment. As I write, AIDS is devastating this nation. The American public, accustomed to scientific discovery (we can solve any problem if we just spend enough money on research), wants a cure or vaccine *now*. People moan when researchers say that discovery of a vaccine could be a decade or more away. In the meantime, people die and dreams are destroyed.

But how many lives have been destroyed because someone has refused to wait?

### The Hazard of Hasty Action

Think back to a launch pad at Cape Canaveral. January 28, 1986. I was there, standing on the beach, impatiently looking at my watch, wondering when the shuttle was going to launch. A few miles down range, a NASA administrator snapped, "My God, Thiokol, when do you want me to launch? Next April?"[2]

A question still lingers in the minds of many Americans: Did impatience lead to the *Challenger* disaster over the Atlantic, shattering the dreams not only of the seven astronauts but also of hundreds of others in the space industry whose futures were tied to a vigorous schedule of space launches?

Most of us are aware of the inherent dangers of impatience. I once wrote an article on the poverty of impatience. The first king of Israel, Saul was an example of that poverty. Early in his reign he had been warned about impatience. But when he assembled the Israelites at Gilgal to fight the Philistines, who outnumbered them, Saul wanted Samuel, the spiritual leader and prophet of Israel, to bless the troops and thus all but guarantee victory. Saul waited seven days.

When Samuel didn't show and recruits began to go AWOL, Saul impulsively decided to offer the sacrifice himself, an unthinkable act. Samuel arrived "as soon as he [Saul] had finished."[3] Saul's brashness caused by his loss of confidence in God and in Samuel eventually put a young shepherd named David on the throne.

Impatience hamstrings many dreams. Patience, however, can turn a dream into reality.

### Dare to Wait

When I think of patience, I naturally think of Mel Fisher of Key West, who defied the Atlantic to recover sunken treasure from the Spanish galleon, *Atocha*. In 1662 the *Atocha* sailed from Havana, carrying 160 pieces of gold bullion, 901 silver ingots, more than 250,000 silver coins, 600 copper planks, 350 chests of indigo, and assorted other items. Destined for Spain and the treasury of King Philip IV, which had been depleted by the expenses of expeditions into Mexico, Colombia, and Peru, the ship sank in fifty-five feet of water, thirty-five miles from Key West. For three hundred years the treasure waited discovery.[4]

Mel Fisher dreamed of that booty.

When he couldn't pay his divers, he promised, "Someday there will be stacks of silver bars lined up like a brick wall. There will be bars of gold and treasure chests." Sure. To many it sounded as if Mel had seen too many movies of the *Raiders of the Lost Ark* variety. Yet many divers were patient with Fisher. Cynics called him a fool; the state of Florida tried to deny his legal rights to the dream; and rival treasure hunters circled him like sharks. For seventeen years he and his crew searched.

During the first two years of the search, his divers found nothing of value. Still, Fisher convinced investors to keep the operation afloat.

In 1971 he found musket balls; in 1973, three, seventy-six-pound silver bars and an anchor. In 1975, his son Kirk recovered nine cannons.

A Key West lawyer named David Paul Horan kept this dreamer afloat legally. Broke and owing buckets of money to Miami and Washington lawyers, Fisher would grin and say, "Today's the day." Sure, Mel.

Then came July 20, 1985, seventeen years after his initial plunge. One radio message changed everything and set the people of Key West dancing up and down Duval Street. Kane Fisher radioed his father, "Put away the charts! Silver bars! We've hit the main pile!"

The jubilant included Fisher "believers," who ranged from those who had bought his yearly offerings of stock at $1,000 a share to a group of investors who had put down $4.6 million. At one time, Fisher signed away 5 percent of the fortune for a mere $9,000, using a table napkin as a contract.

The real heroes were his divers. Although some of them became instant millionaires, they had often gone as long as twenty-four weeks without being paid. One diver, Pat Clyne, had worked twelve years for Fisher. "It's just as though he'd seen it. They said he was luring investors with ridiculous claims, but he was right. . . . Now kids'll grow up on Mel Fisher stories."[5]

What kept those men diving? The promise of riches? No, the power of Fisher's glittering dream. For many divers, Mel Fisher was a twentieth-century Pied Piper. Hundreds of divers had worked for him through the years, "making his dreams theirs. The ones who *hung in* got to see the dream come true," commented Jim Sinclair, a nautical archaeologist.[6]

Somewhere, on the days following July 20, 1985, there were

many divers who cursed their impatience: "Why didn't I stay?" Patience paid off; patience pays off.

In an age captivated by the instant—whether photos or pudding, ice tea or TVs—we have to be patient for our dream. Sometimes it just moseys along at its own speed.

## RESISTANCE FACTOR 2: LACK OF APPRECIATION OF YOUR DREAM

Do you know any of those individuals who "can't seem to find themselves"? Who cannot discover their niche? Who move from one thing to another? Dreamer Mel Fisher started out designing bridges as an engineer in the military. Next, he worked on his father's chicken farm. Then, he opened California's first diving shop in Torrance. All *before* he found his niche in Key West.

Almost every family has one: a ne'er-do-well, one who is always being bailed out.

Politicians become successful once (and if) they can recruit people to their dreams. Some have launched political campaigns that led to careers on five-dollar contributions; some have launched political campaigns on family names. I remember, as a college student in 1968, waiting for hours at the Nashville airport for Robert Kennedy, who had just announced his Democratic candidacy for president. He had electrified our college campus by his decision to run.

Robert Kennedy had an incredible ability to share his dream with others because he appreciated *his* dream.

Yet in all of our lives, there comes a moment when we have to move on to our own dream. Another's dream or a secondhand or hand-me-down dream will not satisfy.

### Don't Settle for a Secondhand Dream

It's easy to "hobo" on another's dream. Riding the rails at seventy-five miles per hour is great, but whose train is it?

Another term for a dreamer who doesn't move on is *parasite,* an organism living in or on another; something dependent on something else for existence or support without making a useful or adequate return. Some people are dreamer parasites, hangers-on. Rather than risk their comfort to pursue their own dream, they choose to live in the shadow of another's dream. Sometimes dreamers do "hobo" on another's dream as a steppingstone to their own dream, however.

I see that with so many of these Elvis Presley look-alikes. I was amazed that during the Statue of Liberty celebration in 1986, they had an Elvis look-alike contest. Many of these look-alikes, who expend excessive energy to win the contests, have musical skills and could make it on their own, but, instead, they hang on to Elvis. What a tragedy! They will never be known for who they are but for who they look like.

### Steppingstone Dreams

I am not certain how I feel about steppingstone dreams in a career path or dream path. I look back at my academic career, five years in college administration. I wonder if I left any lasting contribution to the two institutions from which I received paychecks?

Then I remember struggling with my desire to write—having to give up all the perks and security of a position with a denomination. I had plenty of advice. One man, who had spent a lifetime with a denomination to get his gold watch and pension, now had plenty of time to do the writing he had waited to do. "Go for the security," he advised. "You'll have plenty of time to write *later*." Later? But I wanted to write now.

Another man said, "But wouldn't you hate to come to old age, wondering, 'What if I had risked it back then?' Wouldn't you hate to come to old age, resenting the best years you gave to a corporation?"

Another said, "You're young enough that even if you fail, you can find a good job. Go for it!"

But the one that tipped the scales was the man, who through tears in his eyes, confessed, "I wish that I could do that, but I mortgaged my soul a long time ago."

I realized that even if I failed miserably in the venture, I would at least have the satisfaction of knowing that I had tried *hard*.

Even if I failed, *this* dream deserved a chance. I didn't want to come to my golden years with a burden of regrets or "I-wish-I-had's." I'll choose bruises, first, thank you.

For even bruises can be opportunities.

Your job can be fun, well paying, rewarding, but is it *your* dream? Is it a step closer to your dream? That's why entrepreneurs have become our generation's heroes. Yes, they might have been good—even great—employees at IBM, GE, Xerox. O.K., they might have earned the gold watch and pension after thirty years. But today thousands are cashing in their chips to work harder, longer hours and are certainly under more stress to give their own dream a chance.

Lee Durham, a black New York City policeman, had long wanted to own a McDonald's franchise. He could have put in his years on the force, then retired still a young man, and started a second career under the Golden Arches.

No. Lee wanted to make hamburgers not arrests. He wanted to be in business for himself. He wanted a chance.

McDonald's gave him a chance in Harlem, the only franchise place offered. He would be a guinea pig (along with his $35,000 in life's savings and the bank's $125,000) to test black entrepreneurism.

Many people might like to own a fast-food franchise. But what about their egos? What if a friend were to come in and find them frying burgers because a high schooler did not report to work on schedule? Or in Durham's case, how would he respond if one of the criminals he had arrested came in, looked up, and said, "Hey, aren't you the guy that busted me? You must be down on your luck, frying hamburgers at McDonalds."

Lee Durham was told that he couldn't survive in his Harlem location. Oh yes, he still gets robbed about sixteen times a year, but because of his courage—because of his refusal to settle for a secondhand dream—he now owns seven McDonald's franchises and is president of the National Black McDonald's Proprietors Association. When he opened his store there were only 8 black franchise owners in the McDonald's family. Today, there are 170. Moreover, Durham has been instrumental in helping McDonald's become the largest employer of black youths in the country (currently 17,000) and the largest employer of black accountants. His dream includes plenty of room for others.[7]

## RESISTANCE FACTOR 3: BUSYNESS

Prepackaged, precooked food. Just pop it in the microwave. Automatic dishwashers wash the dishes while you sleep or jog. Permanent press.

America's commitment to leisure keeps a thousand dreamers hopping with products, gadgets, ideas that will save time. A hundred people earn a hundred grand a year teaching time-management techniques. People spend millions for books, schedule calendars, and tapes on how to save time.

"I'd love to, but I'm busy" is as American as apple pie. That slogan would make a fitting epitaph on most of our tombstones. I travel with a green spiral notebook containing a list of things that *absolutely, positively* have to get done today. Another page deals with tomorrow. Another page the next ninety days. Always a list.

Rabbi Harold Kushner reported that he's never had a person on a deathbed say, "If only I could have another couple of hours at the office . . ." Ah, we're never too busy to die.[8]

Death has a way of interrupting our busyness with the eternal. Shouldn't a dream have as much right to intrude as death?

It's possible to be so busy, even if your agenda is packed with good things, that you fail to pursue your dream.

In fact, I suspect that some folks keep busy to drown out the sounds of their souls, the internal stirrings of their dreams. They breathlessly race here and there, making little time for reflection, for hearing their own heartbeats.

I suspect that on some of those dives into the blue waters of the Atlantic, Mel Fisher was able to drown out the critics and cynics and bankers and to hear his own heartbeat, to heed that *Go for it!*

Although I travel about two hundred nights of the year, I still regularly schedule what I call surf time. I need time to hear the waves, to catch some sun, but really time to think—time to disconnect from the frantic busyness of "It's Friday. I'm supposed to be in . . ."

So many would-be dreamers live their lives in an emotional firehall, the alarms continuously ringing.

It's possible to be too pooped to embrace your dream. You can be like a boxer, pleading after the eighth round, "Please don't ring that bell again."

How many would-be artists or writers or singers or whatevers drop into bed exhausted? They cannot possibly give their dream the best.

What a sad commentary: Too busy to dream.

## RESISTANCE FACTOR 4:  POOR PRIORITIES

I like this definition of priority: Any activity containing the *highest* potential for reward. Mel Fisher might have been happy working in that diving shop in Torrance and might have made a good living—*might have*.

Assuming that you have a clear understanding of your dream, keep reviewing your priorities. Keep them on your bathroom mirror, in your daytimer or checkbook; have them calligraphied; carry them in your wallet. Constantly ask yourself these three questions:

- What shall I *do?*
- What shall I *not* do?
- What shall I do *first?*[9]

These questions continuously dominate the thinking of the dreamer.

I read about a diet called the Best Diet. Considering my constant battle with weight, I thought it deserved a try. The Best Diet promises you can eat whatever you want and still lose weight. Got to be a catch somewhere, right?

There is. Whatever you eat has to be the *best.* So you can have a chocolate chip cookie—if it's the best. Therefore, those store-bought packaged cookies are out. They may be good, but they aren't the best.

The principle behind the diet is delayed reinforcement. By saying no to junk calories or even good cookies, I make room for the best.

So it is with life. The best must take priority. Sadly, many Americans sacrifice what they really want for what someone says they should have or should do. People ask about my writing habits: When do I get time to write? Answer: I watch very little TV; I'm not a shopper. The best answer is that I *choose* to prioritize my schedule to make time for writing.

Yes, there are invitations that challenge my priorities, things that would be fun, interesting, more immediately rewarding than the hours at a word processor. However, I refuse to nurture any relationship or invitation that weakens my pursuit of my priorities. Sometimes that means a daily choice. What can I do today about my dream?

## What Should I Do?

You can always find a plastic-coated, see-through envelope in my briefcase. On a piece of paper inside, I have listed my goals. By knowing my priorities, by daily (sometimes hourly) reminding myself of those freely chosen priorities, I have also decided what I should not do. Thus, when an opportunity comes along, I can quickly determine if it has my monogram on it.

## What Should I Not Do?

Several years ago I was asked to write a book about a prominent Washington personality. Wow, was I flattered (for a few days)! But as I carefully examined the offer, I realized that I would be expending my time and my energy (that translates, postponing my dream) to make another's dream come true instead of mine. I said no, nicely.

Less than a year later, I was invited to become an associate of one of America's most famous writers and ministers. My friends were blown away. "Of course you're going to say yes. What an opportunity!" For days I listened to their conviction that "You are on your way. He'll make you somebody." Yet something troubled me about the invitation. I would be paid well, but I would be working primarily to make *his* dream come true.

Then, one afternoon as I wrestled with this "chance of a lifetime," my friend Russ Bredholt asked one well-timed question: "But what about *your* dreams?"

I made a decision that I have never regretted. I said no.

### What Should I Do First?

Now, what about that third question: What to do *first*? Couldn't I have gone with the celebrity and slowly moonlighted my dream? Perhaps. But I suspect that I would have been too exhausted by his dreams to ignite mine.

My life is focused around my priority to write and to speak. Some invitations are good, but many would still distract me from the *best* use of my time and energy.

Every day I ask myself, "What have I done today that has moved me closer to my dream?" That's a good question for you too.

When do you ask it? Well, if you wait until bedtime, the answers will be determined by the question you should have asked yourself just before you put your feet on the bedroom floor to start the day: "What can I do today that will move me closer to my dream?" During your lunch or coffee break, the question will be: "What am I doing today that will move me closer to my dream?" Baby steps in dream making may seem momentarily insignificant but, like a savings account, they do add up.

In playing the childhood game Mother May I?, the distance to the goal is always the same, whether you take baby steps or giant steps or leaps to get there.

Dreamers are not necessarily any smarter or more clever than other people. They do, however, know the preciousness of a time zone called today, and they make the most of it.

Today is a good day to evaluate your dreams.

### RESISTANCE FACTOR 5:  DREAM BUSTERS

Everyone has a dream buster in his or her life. The dream buster is that skeptic who snarls or laughs, "Who, you?" Some dream busters specialize in attacking all dreams; anyone's dream is a potential bull's eye for their attack. Others aim at the dreams of people with the same last name.

Why do they attack dreams? Some have the ashes of their own dreams littered around them. They have embraced failure instead of their dream and have given in to despair. They have thrown in the towel. Or they are jealous. Perhaps they resent your optimism, enthusiasm, the resources you have stockpiled, and think, "If only I had had that, *then* I could have . . ."

Some dream busters are verbal. They lash out at the dreamer. They taunt or tease, even humiliate, forcing the dreamer, like a turtle, back into the dreamshell. Some victims never have the courage to venture out again. The dream is lost, perhaps forever.

Some dream busters are quiet and dignified. They don't tease, taunt, or threaten. They say nothing. They offer no word of encouragement or expression of pleasure with the accomplishments of the dreamer. In 1960 President Dwight Eisenhower, perhaps inadvertently, filled this role in the life of his vice president, Richard Nixon. Nixon had claimed his "experience"—his working one heartbeat from the presidency—as one reason why he should be elected rather than Senator John Kennedy. That seemed a reasonable claim to many voters.

Naturally, reporters asked President Eisenhower about the claim, seeking specific examples of Nixon's leadership and contributions. Ike remarked that he would have to think about it for a week. That offhanded, harmless remark gained quick press attention. If the President couldn't think of an example, Nixon's boast must be an exaggeration. The remark clearly cost Nixon voters and helped contribute to his narrow defeat in 1960.[10]

Dream busters can be mates. Husbands and wives should be mutual encouragers, committed to sharing the dream quest. Unfortunately for every one who says, "I owe all my success to my husband/wife who has stood by me all the way," there are perhaps ten who say, "I did it in spite of him" (or "to spite her").

Divorce courts everyday hear the accusations and counter-charges: "If only you had supported me, I could have . . ." Ellen and David are one example of a couple who lived out this nightmare. Ellen busted her husband's dream.

David dreamed of making it big as a realtor. He worked long, hard hours, slowly building his career in a highly competitive office while Ellen ruthlessly pot-shotted his dream: "But Charles [another realtor in the same office and a close friend of the couple] made $55,000 last year." Next, she daily pointed out that Charley's house was bigger, far more impressive: "Why do we have to live in this dump?"

David resisted her nagging, building his nest egg for a couple of high-risk, big-return deals that Charles wouldn't touch. He tried to explain his long-term strategy to Ellen, but she wanted it *now*.

Eventually, to dampen her criticism, he bought her her dream house. Ellen went on a buying spree (he later called it a rampage) to decorate and furnish the house. The bills were outrageous, and the pressure on David intensified for cash—quick cash.

David struggled with his dream; Ellen stepped up her criticizing and nagging. There was never enough money. She always wanted more. When I get this, she insisted, then I will be happy. Always a *then*.

Suddenly Ellen turned personal, vindictive. She accused him of having an affair with a woman associate in the firm. David panicked. Strapped for cash and worried about his position, he made some bad investment decisions that compromised his realtor's license and reputation. Soon, both of their dreams collapsed around them in a mound of unpaid bills. A divorce followed. Ellen and David could have had it all but ended up with nothing except anger.

At times the dreamer has to ask, "Why am I so willing to allow the dream buster so much power over my dream?" And the one whose dream has collapsed must ask, "How much of the collapse is attributable to the dream buster?" It's tempting to put all the blame on the dream buster.

At times, because of the nature of your relationship to the

dream buster, you have to persevere. At other times you have to move on to another dream.

## Other Family Members

You don't see as many Blank and Sons in today's business world. Today, it would be John Doe *and Offspring*. Yet the reality is that many families cannot work together. Look at the problems with Miss Ellie Ewing's clan.

I think of a family of morticians, who had worked together for two generations. But the third generation of brothers couldn't work together and fulfill their father's dreams. So the younger son left the family firm and opened his own mortuary as a competitor to his own family.

Tom was one of my counselees. He chose me because he thought I would understand since I had been a funeral director. He was an only son. His parents had worked hard to build four funeral homes, assuming that Tom would step into the family business/dream.

But Tom wanted to work with the living, not the dead. So he had to have a dream-busting conversation with his parents. He declared his love for them, his appreciation for all they had done for him, then revealed *his* dream: to be a physician. They were devastated.

It took many conversations—all tense, most long, some loud—to convince his parents that *their* dream was not Tom's dream. Their "But we did this all for you" was not strong enough to dowse his dream, although for many other sons or daughters in similar situations, it would have been. Simply, Tom convinced them that their dream boundaries had intruded on *his* dream turf.

In some families that independence will not bear close examination or scrutiny. Some families have provided trinkets and a lifestyle with strings attached, which manipulate the dreams and choices of a son or daughter.

During the Civil War, many fathers strenuously objected to their daughter's plans to become nurses. "No daughter of mine is going to become a nurse!" was a common declaration. Emily

Parsons was thirty-seven years old when the war broke out. Against her father's strong objections, she volunteered as a nurse. Although she had never been away from home before, Emily now moved to Boston where she trained for eighteen months at Massachusetts General Hospital and excelled. Emily was appointed head nurse on the *City of Alton,* a steamer operated by the Sanitary Commission, which sailed within site of the Confederate stronghold, Vicksburg, in order to take on more than four hundred patients.

She then became the supervisor of nurses at the 2,500-bed Benton Barracks Hospital in St. Louis. Her appointment was considered one of the most important given to a woman during the Civil War. Emily's impressive record as a nurse won her the warm support of the doctors. She helped make nursing a recognized and noble profession for women, though her dream began with a no to her family.[11]

Who knows how many dreams have been suffocated by individuals who worked in the "family business" or who followed their parents' dreams for them?

Paul Ecke, a second-generation American, decided in 1919 to stop working on his father's small dairy farm in Los Angeles. He wanted to concentrate on growing poinsettias, a strange decision given the fragileness of the plant.

Paul had to find frost-free land, with plenty of water and a railroad siding. In the early days, Ecke and his colleagues found it tough going as the poinsettia was very perishable and almost impossible to ship. But years of pursuing the dream led to the Eckespoint, one of the major hybrids.[12] I wonder if poinsettias would be so plentiful at Christmas if Paul had remained in the dairy business?

It is not always a father or mother who resists a dream. Tom Monaghan and his brother pioneered in home pizza delivery. In the early days there were a few problems, to say the least: lawsuits, cold pizzas, irregular paychecks. So Tom's brother quit the struggling enterprise for the security of the U.S. Postal Service. He pawned a dream for "security."

Despite the defection of his brother, Tom Monaghan kept

making and delivering pizzas right into multimillionairedom. Today he not only owns Domino's Pizza but also the Detroit Tigers.[13]

A decision to pursue—or not to pursue—the dream has consequences.

God only knows how many parents through their wills have attempted to meddle in their son's or daughter's life, even from the grave. God only knows how many family gatherings are ruined by loud disagreements over dreams.

Some sons and daughters have misinterpreted the biblical injunction to honor their father and mother. Some have buried their dreams, masking their action (or inaction) with this scripture.

In my own family, my father wanted more for me than the family tradition of working for the Louisville Gas and Electric Company. Three generations of Smiths have worked there. My dad wanted me to be a minister.

My career decision began on a warm September day in 1959, almost twenty years before I cashed my first check as a professional speaker. My junior-high-school principal, Mr. Hatfield, made an announcement that anyone wishing to enroll in the speech club could do so during fourth period in room 201. I can still hear the snickers of some of my macho junior-high buddies when I did that.

I remember getting up at 4:30 A.M. on many Saturdays to ride two or three hours to a speech tournament somewhere in Kentucky while my friends slept. On some of those cold winter mornings, it would have been easy to roll over and go back to sleep. But I made a decision. And my dad never once complained about getting up to take me. He encouraged my dream. Not everyone gets that kind of support. So, sometimes, a dreamer has to listen to the dream more than to family members.

## RESISTANCE FACTOR 6: FEAR

Many dreamers stand at the edge of the dream and wait, afraid to pursue. The pause doesn't refresh, it destroys. The dream loses momentum. Many people ignore the cliche to strike while the iron is hot. Shakespeare said:

> There is a tide in the affairs of men,
> Which, taken at the flood, leads on to fortune.
> Omitted, all the voyage of their life
> Is bound in shallows and in miseries.
> We must take the current when it serves,
> Or lose our ventures.[14]

My counselor friend Sharon Matthews observed, "It is good to have available for other things the space that fear takes up in our lives." Is fear menacing your dreams? Is fear squeezing out your dream? I suppose I could coin the word *dreamaphobia,* but that would only give a name to the pain.

I think of Virginia's Lt. Gov. Doug Wilder, a Democrat and upset winner in 1986. Republican party leaders were convinced that all their candidate had to do to win was to be alive on November 5. The politicos also said Virginians would *never* elect a black man. From the beginning, Wilder was an underdog. In fact, eleven white Democratic leaders urged him not to run, fearing that he would hurt the entire ticket. Wilder had no money and only two full-time staffers, but he had a dream. He had been elected Virginia's first black state senator since Reconstruction. Wasn't that enough for him?

No. As a black, Doug Wilder had been barred admission to the University of Virginia, so he attended all-black Virginia Union. After his graduation in 1951 with a degree in chemistry, he was offered a job with the state health department as a cook. Later, while working as a toxicologist in the state medical examiner's office, he began attending Howard University Law School. His law practice made him a wealthy man, but he was a black man with political ambition in a state that valued tradition.

He won by listening to voters. He traveled on a 3,719-mile auto trip of the state, visiting 338 cities and towns and shaking thousands of hands. He didn't try to guilt whites into voting for him to make up for past injustices. He just shared his dream that he could make a difference as lieutenant governor of Virginia.[15]

Doug Wilder dared to run *toward* his dream.

Your dream deserves your full cooperation. It can't happen without you, nor can it drag you along.

How long have you resisted, even for seemingly good reasons? There will be ample opportunities for you to be baited into abandoning the dream. For example, one bank to which Lee Durham turned for his financing of his franchise was far more interested in how a policeman could accumulate $35,000 in savings than in his dream or potential as a businessman.[16] Doug Wilder had to ignore many slights as a black member of the Virginia legislature. Some would have thrown in the towel, claiming race to be an obstacle. But that would only have made it more difficult for the next dreamer.

Two thousand years ago an old man had a dream and a longing; Simeon was waiting "for the consolation of Israel." To live to see the Messiah was his dream, and he had been promised he would not die until he had seen Him. He must have stared at thousands of babies as he waited for the fulfillment of his dream. It would have been easy to become discouraged. Still, day after day, he went to the Temple, thinking *Today might be The Day!"*

Was there any indication when he awoke that particular morning that that was the day? Would it not have been easy for this old man to roll over and go back to sleep? To mumble, "Tomorrow"? Instead, he went to the Temple and found a young couple coming for the ceremony of purification after the birth of a son.

Simeon went up to Mary and Joseph *at that very moment* and blessed the child and the parents.[17] You see, sometimes it only takes a moment to miss or a moment to resist the dream.

You must learn to control your disappointment so you don't resist your dream, even for a moment. After all, a moment can make a difference.

L. J. Cardinal Suenens once said, "Happy are those who dream dreams and are ready to pay the price to make them come true." Are you resisting paying the price to make your dream come true?

～～～～～～～～～～～～～～～

1. Is it easier for a single adult or a married adult to pursue a dream?

2. What are some ways I have postponed my dream?

3. Do I have a dream that I have passed on that I now regret?

4. If I had been one of Mel Fisher's divers, how would I have explained not being paid in twenty-four weeks?

5. Would I describe myself as patient or impatient for my dream?

6. Do I fully appreciate my dream? If so, what can I offer as evidence?

7. Can I think of an example of a "parasite" dream in my life or a friend's?

8. The author contends that "even bruises can be opportunities." Do I agree or disagree?

9. Why have I been so willing in the past to allow my dream buster so much power over my dream?

10. If I were Tom (page 55), what would I have said to his parents' "After all we've done for you?"

11. How much space does fear take up in my life?

12. Am I willing to pay the price to make my dream come true?

13. If I had been Lee Durham, would I have sunk my life's savings into a McDonald's franchise in Harlem?

14. Is it really possible to be so busy that one can fail to pursue a dream?

15. Are my present priorities encouraging or discouraging my dream?

16. I would identify the following as my time wasters:

17. What have I done in the last twenty-four hours to make my dream happen?

# 4

# PICK YOUR DREAM TURF

All the world's a stage,
And all the men and women merely players:
They have their exits and their entrances;
And one man in his time plays many parts.[1]

Familiar words from Shakespeare introduce the theme of this chapter: staging the dream.

In military terms, a "staging area" is a place where troops are assembled before an assault. Your dream has to have a launching pad. Sometimes the dream turf is an expected location (like Thomas Edison's laboratory); other times it's an unexpected place (like a Birmingham jail or the Lincoln Memorial for Martin Luther King, Jr.).

Jackie Robinson's staging area was the baseball stadium. Professional baseball, before 1947, was a white man's sport. That radically changed in 1945 when Branch Rickey decided to sign a black to a major league contract. His scouts hunted through the "colored" leagues until they found a candidate: Jackie Robinson.

However, not everyone agreed with Rickey's decision. Whenever Jackie came to bat, hostile fans hurled racial slurs. Hate mail increased. Death threats became common. Rumor had it that Jackie slept with the wives of white teammates and that he was spreading contagious diseases among his teammates. Many of his fellow Dodgers were browbeaten with the phrase *nigger lover*.

Ed Charles, the black third baseman on the 1969 World Champion New York Mets team remembered seeing Robinson play:

> Everybody in our part of town wanted to see him. Old people and small children, invalids and town drunks all walked through the streets. Some people were on crutches, and some blind people clutched the arms of friends, walking slowly on parade to that ball park to sit in the segregated section. We watched him play that day and finally believed what we had read in the papers, that *one of us was out there on that ball field*. When the game was over, we kids followed Jackie as he walked with his teammates to the train station, and when the train pulled out, we ran down the tracks listening for the sounds as far as we could . . . . We wanted to be part of him as long as we could.[2]

It was one thing for Robinson to play at Dodger Field in Brooklyn. Thousands of blacks scraped together money from the cookie jars to see history made. But some stadiums were a long way from the "safety" of Brooklyn. Jackie's dream had to be staged in Chicago, in Washington, D.C., in St. Louis. Travel presented unique problems. He was a Dodger but not a Dodger in that he couldn't always stay where the team stayed or eat where the team ate. But he had a dream: to open major league baseball to all.

The second or third time Robinson played a stadium, he began to sense the dream was coming true. There began to be loud cheers when he came to bat, especially from the black fans who had come out to support his dream.[3]

Staging the dream will determine the results. For example, Martin Luther King, Jr., could not have been effective in Spokane, Washington, because the city did not have a significant black population to inspire or a history of racial prejudice to overcome. Thomas Edison could not have chosen a classroom or a church for his scientific experiments. Each found the proper dream turf.

Let's examine your dream turf as you ask yourself the questions that will help you stage your dream.

## WHAT IS MY ARENA FOR ACHIEVEMENT?

Whatever your arena, embrace it. Lyndon Johnson started out in a small rural schoolhouse in Cotulla, Texas, a seemingly unlikely place for the resume of an eventual president of the United States. I am stunned by the number of people who decide "it can't happen *here*." So they put the dream on hold and wait for their *next* appointment, their next promotion. "Ah, then . . ." they reason. Sadly, some people go through an entire lifetime without having touched "then."

### A Succession of Unlikely Arenas

For some, the dream unfolds in a succession of arenas. Take Beverly Sills, for example. One of the best-known opera singers in the world, she was, for a number of years, a wife and mother, juggling a career and family long before that became in vogue. She gave up her overseas singing opportunities because of the strain on her family. But slowly, she resumed her career and sang her way into the hearts of Americans unaccustomed to opera.

Then she retired. Some said the New York City Opera was headed for artistic and financial ruin. Who could replace her? That had been her arena. What would she do next?

Who would have suspected that she would become the general manager of that opera company, now financially "on the ropes." Beverly's first surprise was that the company had no money to meet its payroll. Attendance figures had been inflated; the company had no clear understanding of the audience it was attracting. With almost no business experience she was thrust into the role of "miracle worker" on Sixty-second Street.

Sills saw this as her next arena in which to succeed. She had raised millions of dollars as national chairman of the Mother's

March on Birth Defects; now she took that experience and inserted the word *opera*. She developed the reputation, "She doesn't hesitate to ask!" That meant traveling 250,000 miles a year to keep the stage of the New York City Opera, with 450 artists and hundreds of other staff, lit.[4]

Sills succeeded in going from player to team manager. Her dream has opened doors for hundreds who need an opportunity to chase their dreams for a career in opera.

It's tempting to want another arena. The grass always looks greener on the other side of the fence. However, reality says that grass is always greener where it is watered and fertilized.

Historically, America has been the land in which anyone could stage a dream. First for millions of immigrants. Then for millions of Americans as they followed Horace Mann's advice, "Go west."

When I moved from North Carolina to California in 1977, I drove a comfortable U-Haul truck, stopping in good motels and eating in good restaurants. As I drove, I thought of those Smiths before me, who had traveled West in wagon trains to brave hostile Indians, fever, disease, and weather. Could my courage begin to match theirs?

We no longer look West. We look up, into the heavens. As a generation of boys once dreamed of gold in California, a generation of children, boys *and girls,* now dreams of space exploration.

Ask yourself, "What is my arena?" Then be prepared to accept the answer.

### Unseen Arenas

Sometimes arenas can only be seen in the mind's eye. Margaret Hyer Thomas, daughter of the founder of Southern Methodist University in Dallas, told this story about her father's taking the family for a drive in 1915. "Father took Mother and me out over the narrow dirt road through fields of Johnson grass. On a small incline, he stopped the car and said, 'This is where Dallas Hall will stand.'"

And just how did the founding president's wife react? "She

burst into tears and said, 'You've lost your mind. You can't build a university in the middle of a prairie.'" No one spoke on the way back into Dallas.

But Robert Stewart Hyer saw his arena and would not be deterred. He chose Ivy League colors for S.M.U., hired the architects who had designed Stanford University in California, and directed that the first building resemble Thomas Jefferson's Monticello. Dr. Hyer worked aggressively to find donors who could underwrite his dream, a great Methodist university in Texas.

Today, in that densely populated area of Dallas, one cannot find a blade of Johnson grass. Hyer's dream, Southern Methodist University, dominates the neighborhood.[5]

One expanding dream turf is the military. Maj. James M. Dubik wrote a candid article in *Newsweek,* describing his arrival at West Point to teach. To his surprise he was the one to receive an education from the women cadets. Dubik quickly discovered the inadequacy of his stereotypes about women in the military as expressed here:

> [The women cadets] took themselves and their career futures seriously. They persevered in a very competitive environment. Often they took charge and seized control of situations. They gave orders; they were punctual and organized. They played sports hard. They survived, even thrived, under real pressure. During field exercises, women cadets were calm and unemotional even when they were dirty, cold, wet, tired, and hungry. They didn't fold or give up.

The experience caused Dubik to rethink his expectations for his own two daughters. He listened to their goals and ambitions. Kerith, his twelve year old, said, "I can't imagine not being allowed to do something or be something just because I am a girl."[6]

Your courage could open an arena for a whole new wave of dreamers. Just as Jackie Robinson opened the door for Ed Charles, a little black boy in Daytona Beach, Florida, to have his chance years later in baseball, so Ed Charles pushed open that door even further for the next generation of black athletes.

## SHOULD I RENEGOTIATE MY BOUNDARIES?

When I was growing up, I could play anywhere I wanted, as long as it was *inside* the fence. Amazingly, I always found the most curious things just beyond the fence. Just as there was a fence or boundary for our play in our childhoods, so do we have boundaries for our dream turfs in our adulthoods.

Some settlers moved from New England to Tennessee or Kentucky in the 1780s and 1790s because the eastern seaboard had become too crowded. Then, as more settlers moved into the Kentucky and Tennessee frontiers, other pioneers moved on—too crowded. Today I enjoy being with native Californians, particularly in Los Angeles and Orange County, who can tell me about the days before the developers discovered it. The same is true with Florida, particularly in the citrus groves of central Florida.

Often dreamers renegotiate their boundaries by (1) expanding their boundaries; (2) redefining their boundaries; or (3) equipping themselves as they wait for archaic attitudes to change.

### Expand Your Boundaries

Sometimes you can open the right doors by going in and asking your boss or supervisor for more work or by volunteering, "Let me see what I can do."

How many women executives began their careers by typing, filing, answering phones, and making coffee? Those women paved the way for today's wave of female M.B.A.'s.

Lucille Johnston knows about boundary expansion. Fifty years ago her grandparents urged her parents not to send Lucille to high school "because girls just get married and have babies." So she went to work for RivTow Straits, Ltd., a Vancouver-based company (marine transportation / shipyards / heavy equipment). Lucille did everything from dispatching tugboats to purchasing and accounting. In 1948 her boundaries

were stretched when she was assigned to supervise engine re-
pairs. She gained mechanical know-how by reading books on
diesel engines and asking questions, ignoring comments of
male workers who at times were helpful to her.

In the 1950s she spent five years in night school earning a
business degree. She explained her attitude on boundaries: "I
worked for two gentlemen who never restricted me. I was able
to negotiate anything, be it a towing contract or the acquisition
of a company." Today Lucille Johnston is president of a firm
with 1,500 employees and annual sales of $250 million.[7]

## Redefine Your Boundaries

Some people use orthodox or traditional patterns to make
their dreams happen. Others redefine the roadmap.

Perhaps you've "experienced" a Mrs. Fields' cookie from the
largest fresh-baked cookie company in the world. Through
Mrs. Fields' Cookies, thousands of Americans have been introduced to and become fans of macadamia nuts. How did Fields
learn about macadamias (to say nothing of making such great
cookies)? On a vacation to Hawaii, she tasted macadamias, fell
in love with them, and "renegotiated her boundaries" to add
macadamia cookies and brownies to her stores' menus.

In the late nineteenth century an Australian arrived in Hawaii
with a pocketful of seeds which he planted. Initially, the trees
were thought purely ornamental, until the boundary of their
use was stretched. The University of Hawaii developed a macadamia research program to support the fledgling industry. But
none of this might have happened if Dr. John Macadam hadn't
been curious about what the nut tasted like.

When Mrs. Fields' Cookies ran short of macadamia nuts, it
experienced a 6 to 8 percent loss in revenues. So Debbie Fields
expanded her vision. She had to become more than a baker and
a cookie distributor. Debbie bought her own macadamia nut
processing plant in Hawaii in 1985 to insure that her dream
would continue.[8]

**Wait for Attitudes to Change**

Renegotiating the boundaries means coming to terms with *no* and *maybe* and giving yourself time. Bridgette Denevir is a flight training standards instructor for Pan American Airlines, holding licenses as a commercial pilot and as an aircraft mechanic. When she was young, she was told that little girls became stewardesses and little boys became pilots. Cultural boundaries formed those roles then.

So she started accumulating flight time on cargo airlines in the Caribbean and Africa. Meanwhile, she studied maintenance and worked related jobs, such as aircraft sales and service. After a stint in the U.S. army, she earned her private pilot's license in 1978; seven years later her boundary lines included a commercial pilot's license.

It took eleven years to expand her boundaries, but now she is a pilot and an expert on the A–310 Airbus. She did not allow a no to limit her vision or keep her from renegotiating her boundaries.[9]

## WHAT WILL I HAVE TO OVERCOME?

The three previous dreamers have had to overcome their sex. Others have had to overcome their race. Some have had to overcome physical handicaps. Some have had to overcome poverty. Some have had to overcome educational barriers. Some have had to overcome religious barriers. Some have had dual barriers to overcome.

Joseph Kennedy had a dream. He dared to believe that his third-generation American son, Joe, Jr., could become the first Catholic president of the United States. That would not be an easy task since many people assumed a Catholic's first loyalty was to the pope. Moreover, Joe Kennedy had a fair understanding of prejudice. He had overcome his Irish background in the Boston political and social structure to marry Rose Fitzgerald, daughter of the mayor of Boston.

When Joe, Jr., was killed in World War II, the dream might

have ended, but the mantle was passed. Now it would be up to John F. Kennedy to fulfill his father's dream. On Thanksgiving Day, 1956, father and son had a long talk at the family home in Hyannis Port, Massachussets. John presented all the arguments why a Catholic could not be elected president while his dad pooh-poohed every one: his youth, his lack of support from the Democratic party powerbrokers, and his faith.

Kennedy told his son:

> Just remember, this country is not a private preserve for Protestants. There's a whole new generation out there, and it's filled with the sons and daughters of immigrants from all over the world. Those people are going to be mighty proud that one of their own is running for president. And that pride will be your spur; it will give your campaign an intensity we've never seen in public life.[10]

John Kennedy had a tough battle to win the nomination. He had to survive a critical meeting in Dallas with pastors of Protestant churches. He had to win the nomination of his party from a consummate politician with a million IOUs, the senate majority leader, Lyndon Johnson. Then he had to accept Johnson on his ticket, all before facing the vice president, Richard Nixon. But Kennedy won a close election in 1960. On January 20, 1961, at his inauguration, people saw tears glistening in Joseph Kennedy's eyes as he watched his son John, an Irish Catholic from Boston, take the oath of office. Joseph Kennedy was more than just a proud papa.[11] He was a dreamer tasting victory.

Franklin Delano Roosevelt governed this nation from a wheelchair, yet few people considered him handicapped. When he came down with polio at age thirty-nine, a battle erupted between his protectionist mother, Sara Delano, who wanted him to give up his dreams, and Eleanor, his wife, who encouraged his dreams. Only his legs were affected, she argued, not his brain nor his spirit.

For seven years FDR threw himself into his recovery. He

spent all his time exercising and exploring new cures. He dreamed of walking unaided the length of his Hyde Park driveway.

That never happened.

When he decided that he had reached his plateau, he turned his attention to politics. How could he function in the tough world of politics with his handicap? He had the steel braces painted black; he wore his trousers long to hide the braces when he sat down. He had wheels put on a kitchen chair so that he could avoid a wheelchair. He trained, first, his sons and, later, Secret Service agents, to support him so that he could appear to be standing. He had ramps built and elevators installed in buildings where he worked. As president, he had an informal understanding with photographers that no one would shoot him in an undignified position. If anyone did, the Secret Service confiscated the film.

Recently, Hugh Gregory Gallager published a biography, *FDR's Splendid Deception,* about the man who refused to discuss his disability with those closest to him, who insisted that "next year I will be walking."[12] Always "next year."

FDR's courage encouraged and motivated others who were physically handicapped to explore their arenas. On November 6, 1986, Bob Wieland finally crossed the finish line of the New York Marathon, 19,413th. However, Bob was the first person to run the marathon with his arms instead of his legs. Bob Wieland, a veteran who lost his legs in Vietnam, invested 4 days, 2 hours, 48 minutes, and 17 seconds. Why? "For the same reason as 20,000 other people. It's the greatest marathon in the country."[13]

Wieland had three agendas: to expose his born-again Christian faith; to test his physical conditioning; and to promote the President's Council on Physical Fitness. In 1982 he started, and later finished, a 2,784 mile Walk for Hunger across the continent. Three days later, San Diego Chargers head football coach Al Saunders read a newspaper clipping that described Weiland's feat to his players before their game with the Denver Broncos.

Weiland's dreaming influenced the lowly Chargers to come out of the locker room and defeat the division leaders, snapping an eight game losing streak.[14]

Or what about Jeff Keith, who lost his right leg to cancer at age twelve. Inspired by the Canadian amputee, the late Terry Fox, Jeff organized a run through the heartland of America, stopping to visit cancer patients along the way. There were incredible financial and administrative hassles until United Van Lines bought into the dream as a sponsor and provided Jeff and his team with a thirty-foot R.V. motor home and funds.

The run resumed. Jeff averaged nineteen miles a day. Despite the rain, sleet, and snow, he reached Los Angeles in February 1985. He had run 3,300 miles, lost fifty pounds, and worn out forty-five pairs of racing shoes. But Jeff had touched a nerve in many Americans. He had proved that a person with a dream and some semblance of belief in that dream could accomplish almost anything.[15]

The inventory of obstacles must be faced honestly and analyzed before it can be surmounted. But obstacles can become the raw materials that form the dream legends in this country.

## IS MY CURRENT JOB A BOOSTER OR A BARRIER?

Dreams cost money, sometimes lots of money. Not everyone will attract a United Van Lines to underwrite their dream. For some of us, a job helps keep the body and soul together while we chase this portion of the dream.

Consider Robert Johnson of Johnson & Johnson. His dream trail started when he was a teenage apprentice in a Poughkeepsie, New York, apothecary. Then he moved into a partnership in Brooklyn: Seabury *and* Johnson.

Eventually he convinced his two brothers, who knew nothing about pharmaceuticals, to join the company. James had been trained to be a civil engineer and Mead, an attorney. Yet their combined backgrounds in sales, engineering, and law were crucial in the ultimate development of Johnson & Johnson, one of the world's leading pharmaceutical firms.[16]

A dreamer wastes no experience. Present jobs can be intersections where you meet future partners or possibilities. Paint was not ready-mixed before the 1870s. You bought the ingredients and mixed them yourself. Two men, whose companies had business connections, met and listened to each other's dreams. Henry Alden Sherwin worked for a Cleveland firm that manufactured paint. Edward Porter Williams owned part of a Kent, Ohio, glass factory.

With a spirit of adventure, the two men, both in their twenties, sought a challenge. Sherwin's ideas about ready-mixed paint fit the bill. Williams put up $2,000 and his marketing skills. By 1905 Sherwin-Williams paint was launched with its Cover the Earth trademark.[17] Their current jobs launched their dream.

Others have discovered that sometimes you have to move on. The invisible ladder must be climbed, rung by rung.

Ask yourself these questions about your current job:

- What motivated you to choose this company?
- What motivates you to stay at this job?
- Does your job bring you a sense of self-esteem?
- Does your job provide an opportunity for growth and development?
- Do you feel capable of handling more challenging work than what you are currently doing?
- Does your work cause you to compromise any of your values?
- Do you feel that you are worth more than you are being paid?
- If financial security were not a factor, would you continue doing what you are doing?

Those can be tough questions, especially for individuals who have bought the option for the gold watch and who have become comfortable with the trinkets that corporations can offer. Yet it's like that line in the Tennessee Ernie Ford song "Sixteen Tons": "'Saint Peter don't you call me, cause I can't go. I owe my soul to the company sto'.'"

Do you owe your soul to your company? In today's business world of takeovers, plant closings, mergers, that could be risky.

How tragic to come down to the end of one's working career, filled with regrets, with "I should have's." That was the option I faced when I chose to leave my denominational post .with its salary, secretary, fringe benefits, pension, insurance, to be on my own.

Yes, I sensed the need, but then many people have sensed a need. I was willing to risk. How many employees have been told at a farewell party either "I wish I could do what you are doing" or "You'll regret it"?

Our generation has been raised with a safety-net complex. We had netting around our playpens and now we want netting under our economic trapezes. It's not so hard to walk a trapeze *if* the safety net under it is wide enough and you don't ask me to walk without one. That's why I admire the window washers for corporate skyscrapers that dot the urban skylines. That's not for me!

Yet I suspect most of them would not want my job or my dream. Sitting at a word processor for long hours, writing, preparing lectures, answering letters, juggling details, knowing that a group could cancel the speaking engagement at the last minute, could be a type of financial insecurity to them. That's why some people cannot make it in sales. They need a salary and benefits blanket to maintain their economic comfort zone.

But there is an adrenal high that only dreamers can experience. It's an incredible sensation that leads many to sell a company or a project and start over again.

Sobel and Sicila have found the current American fascination with the word *entrepreneur* amusing proof that most people don't understand American history. They argue that entrepreneurs have occupied center stage of American economics and history since the beginning.

Before either Virginia or Massachusetts were colonies, they were companies in which English investors risked their incomes, and in some cases their lives, to create a better life. People endured all sorts of hardships to test themselves against the elements in America. "The American soil proved fertile ground for developing new businesses, based on minerals from aluminum to zinc, for manufactured goods from corn flakes to computers, and for services from small shops to financial supermarkets."[18]

These pioneers saw challenges and opportunities where their families and peers saw nothing. They had a unique ability to recognize the opportunities erupting or slowly evolving from changed circumstances, such as from war. Some helped create the opportunities (or the policies that engineered the opportunity). They risked their fortunes, their personal lives, their families, but generally only after they found ways to make the risks "acceptable" or "manageable."

Americans are still committed to pioneering. In 1985 new business incorporations reached a record 669,000 (29 percent above the level five years previously). Women now own 20 percent of businesses. The Small Business Administration estimates that small businesses have been responsible for more than half of all innovations in new products and services since World War II. In a world of corporate giants there's still room for the small business with the big dream.[19]

Many of them had a boost from a job. Others chose to take the barriers and learn from them. A survey of collegiate business programs points to the growing expansion of entrepreneurial programs. Women, minorities and immigrants, and the young are composing this new group of business dreamers who are suggesting "you can take this and . . ."

## HOW WILL MY DREAM INFLUENCE MY LIFESTYLE?

Dreams do have consequences, positive and negative, immediate and long range, obvious and subtle.

Scully Blotnick, in his book *Ambitious Men,* said that Americans have four primary criteria for evaluating a person's success: fortune, fame, power, and prestige. Many of America's greatest entrepreneurs were once financial poverty cases. The hard work that ultimately led to their dream's success also influenced their social standing.[20]

Jesus understood that reality. He asked, "What will it profit a man if he gains the whole world, and loses his own soul? Or what will a man give in exchange for his soul?"[21] Simply, there's more to having it all than having it all. Many people have reached their dreams but have not found the happiness they expected.

You, as a dreamer, must be careful that your criteria of success are not measured by the trinkets of our materialistic mindset.

Harold Kushner raised this important point in his book *When All You've Ever Wanted Isn't Enough*. He quoted an old rabbi, who asked, "But isn't it possible that those blessings (that you so crave) are behind you, that they are looking for you, and the more you run, the harder you make it for them to find you?" Kushner added, "Isn't it possible indeed that God has all sorts of wonderful presents for us . . . but we in our pursuit of happiness are so constantly on the go that He can't find us at home to deliver them?"[22]

## CONCLUSION

Dreams happen in particular moments, in particular places, in particular circumstances to particular people. Some would argue that the day of dreaming is over, as if America had used up its quota. Boone Pickens, the oil tycoon, observed:

> I have always believed in the ability of talented, motivated young people, and I am optimistic about the future. A new breed of American business and politics is motivated by the same ideals that made this country what it is, ideals that are sometimes dimmed but that always reassert themselves. That new breed will lead us toward success, and that's a story as old as the country.[23]

Your dream can be moved from the darkened stages on the back corridors of your brain or heart to the well-lighted stage of possibility and potential. The stage is there; we're waiting for you, the actor, to begin.

1. What is my arena for achievement?

2. Then what is my launching pad for my dream?

3. If it seems an impossible launching pad, am I giving it a fair chance?

4. Should I renegotiate my boundaries?

5. Do my boundaries need to be expanded? If so, how?

6. What will I have to overcome to make my dream a success?

7. Can I turn the obstacles or handicaps into my advantage?

8. Is my current job a booster or a barrier?

9. How will my dream influence my lifestyle?

# 5

# DARE TO LAUNCH YOUR DREAM

The headlines "If you can dream it, you can do it" in *USA Today* immediately captured my attention. The Prudential Insurance Company ad centered on a car on a lucite road, leading upward to the moon. "Now there's no limit to your ability. To create, to build, to dream."[1] Someone has said a picture is worth a thousand words. Well, that ad was worth a chapter or more of my words.

In the same special section, General Motors Acceptance Corporation described their company as "an official sponsor of American dreams." GMAC should know. It was something for automobile dreamers like Henry Ford, Ransom E. Olds, and Louis Chevrolet to build their cars while people scoffed that horses and carriages would last forever.

Ford's neighbors called him "Mad Henry" when he dared predict that someday almost everyone would own a car. Ford's dream—a car in every driveway—could only be realized if other dreamers could devise a system to help people pay for the cars, primarily on credit. That's why every month I write out a check designated "car payment."

GMAC's ad pictured an elderly man holding a diaper-clad baby. The ad read, "Who says dreams don't come true? You know better."[2] I watched my father at age seventy-six hold his great-granddaughter Martina, on his lap. My dad was living in a world that would have been impossible for him to imagine when he had been her age. Yet what lies ahead for Martina? *Dreams.*

Go back to the opening line of this chapter: *If you can dream it, you can do it!* That seems to be a path from point A—dreaming—to point Z—achieving. However, realistically there are a lot of right turns, left turns, and U-turns between those two points.

Obviously, in our day it takes more than dreaming. There is no shortage of inspiration in this country; there does seem to be, however, a shortage of perspiration. In order to win the jackpot in Las Vegas, you still have to put in that first coin.

A lot of people have stored their dreams or placed them on hold. Noble dreams perhaps, yet untested. You have to release the dream. That takes a lot of courage because the dream could fail and Americans do not have a high appreciation for failure. Few books in bookstores or on the *New York Times* best-selling list have the word *failure* in the title.

"When are you going to do something about your dream?" is a common question today. The answer "one of these days" is equally common. For too many of us, one of these days never comes or we spend a lifetime waiting for an extraordinary day to launch our dream.

Let's examine the five steps in launching a dream.

## STEP 1:  DARE TO PURSUE

Although many people have dreams, few aggressively pursue the dream. For example, a lot of men in 1925, 1926, 1927 dreamed of flying across the Atlantic Ocean.

It's one thing to talk a dream; another, to do a dream.

Hotel owner Ray Orteig turned up the heat under the dreamers by offering a $25,000 prize for the first one to fly nonstop across the Atlantic. As a result, on New York's Long Island, at Roosevelt and Curtiss fields, every day during the months of September and October of 1926, the dreamers and their financial backers paced, one eye on the winds, one eye on their fragile airplanes. The great Richard Byrd, who had conquered Antarctica, headed one team. René Fonck, legendary flying ace of World War I, headed another.[3]

Into that arena stepped an unlikely competitor, Charles Lindbergh, a mail pilot who flew between Chicago and St. Louis. The widest body of water he had flown across was the Mississippi River. What made him think he could fly the Atlantic Ocean?

During that fall of 1926, when Lindbergh thought his time was running out, the newspapers were filled with reports on Fonck, who spared no expense. His plane had been upholstered in leather and supplied with two radios and a bed in order to carry four crewmen. Fonck, a proud Frenchman, was determined to launch his dream—to fly nonstop to Paris—in style.

Unfortunately, the three-engined plane never made it off the runway. On September 21, 1926, it crashed at the end of the runway and burst into flames. Although Fonck survived, two of his crewmen died.[4]

Although other men were not unwilling to dare to pursue their dreams, they were reminded of the perils of adventure. The incident affected Lindbergh's thinking. He scrutinized every detail of the crash and concluded that he had to fly alone. It was one thing to risk his life to launch his dream, but it was something else to risk the lives of other men. He dared to question what some considered to be essential for such a flight. He could enjoy "style" after the flight.

He studied the checklists of a plane's equipment. Which instruments were absolutely necessary? Which were questionable? Lindbergh eliminated the night-flying equipment because of the weight. He scrapped the gauges on the gas tanks, which were heavy and rarely worked, because he could figure the gas usage with his grandfather's watch. He swapped the radio for an extra ninety pounds of fuel. He even ripped extra pages out of his notebook and cut holes of areas in the charts over which he would not fly.

Today we take aviation for granted—we just get on a plane

and take off. But you need to understand that, in 1926, flying was extremely dangerous. Lindbergh had to eliminate ounces, not just pounds. Every ounce lighter, an ounce of gasoline more to slightly reduce the risk of running out of fuel. What about supplies for an emergency landing? he was asked repeatedly.

"If I get to Paris, I won't need any, and if I don't get to Paris, I won't need any either."

He even refused to carry a pound of mail. Lindbergh had to reduce his plane's weight to below the normal take off weight of that day. Fonck's crash had made an impression on the young mail pilot.[5]

Eight precious months passed; any day could be the day that someone beat Lindbergh to the prize. He couldn't wait much longer.

Then, on May 12, 1927, Lindbergh landed at Curtiss Field, Long Island, having tested his plane in its maiden flight from San Diego. En route he set a new lapsed flying time record for a flight across the United States: twenty-two hours.[6] Often small dreams are achieved en route to our big dream.

That day's equivalent of a media blitz developed. Unfortunately much of the news was inaccurate and focused on the danger of the upcoming trip, so Lindbergh's mother came from Detroit to New York to talk to her son about this dream of his. Once she arrived in New York, however, she quickly discovered that her son Charles was the talk of the town. Who did this young unknown midwesterner think he was, to come from nowhere to challenge the greatest flyers in the world and their great planes? What a dreamer! Yet nothing and no one, even his mother, could dissuade Lindbergh from pursuing this dream.

On May 19, after a week of bad weather, Lindbergh decided to relax by taking in a Broadway show. En route to Broadway, he called the weather bureau for an update. The weather forecast predicted that skies would soon clear over the Atlantic. In that moment, Charles Lindbergh recognized his "now." He raced back to the airfield and ordered his plane readied, believing that by dawn, weather conditions would be right for his attempt.

By morning everything was in place. Lindbergh shook hands with his friends, crawled in, started the engine, and taxied to the end of the runway.

He paused before takeoff. There was still time to change his mind. Some moments we sit on the edge of life or death. Police, firemen, medical attendants, and reporters watched the *Spirit of St. Louis*. Lindbergh realized that no one would blame him if he waited; no one would doubt his courage. He said, "Sitting in the cockpit . . . the conviction surged through me that the wheels *will* leave the ground, that the wings *will* rise above the wires, that it is time to start the flight."

At 7:52 A.M. the *Spirit of St. Louis* lifted from the runway, destination Paris. A group of Lindbergh's supporters screamed, "By God, he made it!" [7] It was not a curse but a recognition of the truth: God had given Lindbergh and his plane a chance.

All dreamers have moments of hesitation, not unlike the young child anxious to go off the diving board and into a swimming pool on a hot summer day. That brief moment of hesitation on the edge of the board makes a difference in whether the child falls into the pool or dives into the pool.

## STEP 2: EVALUATE YOUR RESOURCES

Dreamers need to inventory their resources. The Japanese have a system called *kanban,* which provides for the supplies needed today and only today. This system eliminates costly stockpiling. Some dreams, like manufacturing processes, need component parts. Thus your dream will be delayed until the parallel developments are made.

For example, look at the microwave oven. That invention couldn't evolve until a scientist named Palmer Derby developed the continuous-power magnetron. During World War II the idea of a microwave oven became a luxury. Years passed and the idea of a microwave gathered dust until the mid-1950s when Percy Spencer cooked an egg on a prototype before a startled board of directors and won more research money. The problem was that in 1955, when Tappan sold its first microwave, the oven cost $1,295 and was as large as a refrigerator. [8] More technological dreams were necessary before the microwave won its way into the hearts of the American public.

The process of a dream launch is like that of a pebble tossed into a pond; its ripples touch a wide shoreline. The bigger the rock, the bigger the effect.

What are some resources? As a writer, I need libraries. That's one reason I live in Kansas City; the library resources of the area colleges and universities are immense. States like Colorado are creating zones, such as the Denver High Tech Center, to move dreamers and entrepreneurs into the same neighborhood. Thus, one person's accomplishments touch the shorelines of another person's.

Resources can be disguised. They can come from almost un-expected sources. Black people in Little Rock, Arkansas, had long dreamed of a quality education for their children in their lifetimes. This required equal access and equal opportunity. The federal courts agreed with the dream. However, the courage of President Eisenhower was necessary to implement the dream. He ordered federal troops into the city to make sure that the dream was achieved in an orderly manner, to make sure that demagogues didn't spoil the dream. His action and courage later encouraged President John F. Kennedy to order the governor of Alabama, George Wallace, to "step aside" so that James Meredith, a black, could be admitted to the University of Alabama to have access to his dream resources.

What resources are available to underwrite your dream? Do you need to wait for new resources to become available?

## STEP 3: FACE THE BARRIERS

What are the barriers to your dream? Sex? Timing? Age? Money? Lack of education? Family responsibilities? Barriers can be visible or invisible. The most vicious barrier may be in your mind.

I remember when I taught in a ghetto school, making about eight thousand dollars a year (after six years of college and graduate school), I dreamed of writing. Every day after school, I came home to a typewriter and pounded out my dreams and frustrations. I read every story I could that described authors' lifestyles. I daily mouthed my "if only's."

I faced the problem a lot of would-be writers face—getting my foot in the door of the publishing world. Today, when I lecture at writers' conferences, I meet a lot of students whose dreams are blocked by reality. They talk excitedly about "my book." Some even share stories of the projected difference their books will make—"I'll be on Donahue . . ." Fantasies are necessary to keep a novice writing on tough days.

I, however, believe in apprenticeship. Thus, I paid my dues by writing articles long before I attempted a book. Yes, it was a slow, but necessary, grinding progression toward book publication.

Some people, I suspect, would rather *have written* than to write.

Physical handicaps are no longer barriers. We are familiar with sidewalk ramps to expedite access for the physically impaired. At a college concert, I applauded when four male members of the choir lifted another member in his wheel chair onto the risers. His voice was not impaired, only his legs.

One of the most fascinating stories of barriers overcome focuses on Hung Dinh Vu, a young navy ensign. At Pensacola Naval Air Station Hung went through routine physical exams which revealed, unfortunately, that his thigh length, measured from buttocks to knee, was *three-eighths* of an inch below navy standards. So he was rejected for pilot training. Others would have been devastated; Hung challenged the standards. The 21.9-inch minimum upper leg measurement ensured that a pilot could reach an aircraft's rudder pedals and fit properly in an ejection seat. But could anyone be rejected from a dream because his bottom was too small?

Hung, who had escaped from Vietnam after the fall of Saigon, embarked on a pasta-filled diet to add, in his words, "a little more upholstery back there and put the problem behind me."

Meanwhile, some other problems developed to postpone his dream. Many people would have considered the combination of barriers insurmountable. Not Hung. He could not get a security clearance because his two brothers were still in Vietnam, a Communist country. In time, they escaped and another barrier was eliminated.

Then Hung developed a weakness in his eyes and again faced tough navy standards. This time, however, he was able to secure a waiver.

Perhaps the most traumatic event, however, was the death of his mentor and first flight instructor. Was flying worth risking one's life? After reflection, Hung answered yes.

How could one person overcome so many barriers? By taking them one at a time. On June 19, 1987, Vu got his wings as a navy aviator. He never accepted the barriers as permanent. "I always saw me here in this winging [ceremony]."[9] He focused on the future not on the barriers. Fortunately for many of us, handicaps are no longer seen as permanent barriers.

Barriers may be financial. Legions of would-be playwrights, dancers, novelists, musicians work as waiters as they wait for their overdue dreams. Unfortunately, some are so tired by their job, they have little energy left to invest in their art.

If your barriers are financial, you may need to consider one of two options: mortgaging or borrowing.

## Dare to Mortgage

It's one thing to have a dream; most people do.

It's one thing to try the dream; many do.

It's something else to "mortgage" what you have, for something you *might* achieve. *Might*.

I borrowed a lot of money to go to college. I became the first member of my family to graduate from college, but my dream required graduate school, which meant borrowing more money. Although I had a graduate scholarship, I needed living expenses. My senior year in undergraduate school I had worked forty hours a week. But graduate work would require my full attention. I had been selected to serve on a missionary project in Belize, Central America, during the summer before I began graduate work, and this project also required that I pay my own expenses. Yet my participating made sense for my career objectives.

Since the Vietnam War was in full swing, to stay out of school a year and work was to risk being drafted. I made an appointment with Dr. D. D. Holt, president of Scarritt College, to explain my financial problems. When we met, he focused on what a Scarritt education could do for me. He suggested that I borrow the money, but I expressed my reluctance to go deeper into debt.

"Would you feel bad about not paying cash for a car?" he asked.

"No," I answered.

"So you would borrow money for a car that will rust out and depreciate?"

"Yes," I answered.

"Would you feel bad about borrowing money to buy a house?"

"No."

"In fact, if you saved money until you could afford a house, you might never own a home. Isn't that true?" he asked intently.

I had to agree with his logic.

"Ah," Dr. Holt grinned, sensing the closing of a sale. "Then why would you hesitate to invest in your brain? Something in value beyond comprehension or calculation. Something that will help you make the money you need for the essentials in life?"

Needless to say, I borrowed more money, earned a master's degree, and moved on. Later, when I attended Peabody College, I borrowed more—money to be paid back, with interest, but money that financed my dream.

Yes, it would have been great on those first jobs not to have had the loan payments each month. But I reminded myself that I would not have been in a classroom or in a dean's office of a college without having used someone else's money.

My story is repeated by hundreds of architects, engineers, doctors, lawyers, and ministers.

Sometimes mortgaging may be the only way to keep your

dream afloat. But mortgaging may pave the way to illustrate your commitment to others. It may prime the pump. Lindbergh himself put up $2,000 to get his *Spirit of St. Louis* off the drawing boards, through the Ryan factory in San Diego, and finally, in the air headed toward Paris.

It's easy to look over the fence and covet the resources of another dreamer. Lindbergh had to contend daily with the newspaper reports of the French war ace René Fonck, who had not only the plane but also the name to raise a seemingly bottomless pool of money, as well as the curiosity of the American public. Meanwhile, as Lindbergh scrambled to find resources to compete, he realized how far behind Fonck he was. He appreciated the significance of Fonck's substantial headstart. "A lot of people want to be the first to make the nonstop New York–Paris flight," Lindbergh wrote. "It looks as though my idea will end up as it began—a dream."[10] However, the first nonstop New York–Paris flight was Lindbergh's dream, and he persisted. People still have to mortgage in order to launch their dream. It's as American as apple pie.

Nicolette Johnson had burned out after teaching second grade for eight years in one of the worst neighborhoods in Los Angeles. Reading a book called *The Cinderella Complex* changed her life. "I'm just like these women," she said to herself, "unmarried, no children, unhappy on my job, waiting for Prince Charming to rescue me. I have to do something."

So she decided to go back to school for a master's degree in counseling and for certification as a marriage and family counselor. She made some choices: (1) she sold her interest in a house; (2) she cashed in her California teacher's retirement; and (3) she paid off her car loans while paring down her standard of living.

Nicolette went back to waitressing one to two nights a week and on weekends. However, the degree and the state certification required hundreds of hours of fieldwork and supervised counseling, so she again tightened the belt economically.

What kept her from throwing in the towel? "I knew that I was on the right track. I absolutely loved what I was doing. For the first time in years I felt like I was learning, growing and being challenged."[11]

### Dare to Borrow

"Never borrow money needlessly" was the commercial of a popular finance company when I was growing up. When many people found themselves unable to make ends meet, they turned to finance companies.

What is the difference between mortgaging and borrowing? Actually, mortgaging is borrowing on assets you already own, such as property or stocks. Borrowing is often based on what you hope to earn.

Debt has become a way of life for Americans. We amuse ourselves believing that we have "clout" because of a slip of plastic we carry in our wallets. But wise debt can make a dream come true.

Your dream may require heavy borrowing. Nicolette Johnson eventually had to borrow $5,000 in student loans. Hundreds of doctors graduate from medical school owing multiples of Nicolette's investment.

Nicolette is now a school psychologist and part-time junior college counselor who earns approximately $36,000-plus per year. Is she happy? You bet. "I'm doing what I want and my professional responsibilities are limitless. This career is a perfect fit. I've found my niche, and it was worth all the heartache and hassles."[12] The key is in knowing when and how to borrow and in never borrowing needlessly.

Gus Poulis faced the same intersection in 1981, as treasurer of Bleyer Industries, a company that made and sold specialty papers, such as candy wrappers. Poulis discovered that his boss, Lewis Bleyer, wanted to sell out and retire. An accountant, Poulis knew the company would be a good buy for someone. However, Poulis also realized that he would be out of a job as soon as the new owners picked his brains. What could he do to insure his own future?

He first took stock of his finances. After thirteen years at Bleyer, he had $100,000 worth of company stock and a sliver of a dream. Along with three other executives, he approached Congress Financial Corporation and raised $5 million to buy the company. When that investment worked out well, Poulis bought out his partners. Today Poulis has controlling interest in a company with annual sales of $20 million.

Was Poulis exceptional? No. More executives could do the same. Barbara Kallen, a consultant on such acquisitions, observed, "While many managers know the business like the backs of their hands, they don't have the faintest idea of how to go about buying" the business.[13]

That's where creative borrowing comes in. The difference between dream and reality may be the resources that someone else owns and is willing to loan to you.

## STEP 4: BE OPEN TO TEAMING UP WITH SOMEONE ELSE

A proverb suggests, "Five of you shall chase a hundred, and a hundred of you shall put ten thousand to flight."[14] Simple math would question that equation. In the first equation each man put twenty to flight. In the second equation each man put a hundred to flight. Linking up increases productivity and effectiveness. Many dreams have remained mere dreams because a dreamer refused to cooperate with another dreamer. His or her dream wasn't big enough for a partner. *My* dream precluded the thought of *our* dream.

Partnership is a popular concept in business today. Some business risks are too big for a single company or even a giant corporation to risk. So they form a partnership to share the risk.

Think of your dream. Could another person be the energizer that would turn your dream into a reality? As early as 1895, C. S. Rolls, the dashing son of an English baron, raced cars and sold Belgium and French automobiles to his wealthy English friends. If it had wheels and a motor, Rolls was interested in it. His name would not have been associated with excellence and luxury today, however, if he had not met Henry Royce.

In 1884 Henry Royce, an engineer, found himself without a job when his employer went out of business. So he borrowed some money and started his own firm, F. H. Royce, Ltd., to make lamps, cranes, and other electrical devices. His strict attention to detail soon built his reputation. In 1902 he bought a French car; he "deserved" it for his hard work. That car, however, like most cars at the time, was unreliable, loud, and uncomfortable, which irritated the perfectionist Royce.

In a small area of his shop, he began fiddling with a dream: a sturdy two-cylinder car with a perfectly balanced crankshaft to minimize noise and vibration. He built three prototypes, one of which he sold to Henry Edwards.

Henry Edwards had a friend, C. S. Rolls. His first look at the "Roycemobile" overwhelmed him. Somewhat nervously, Rolls met Royce. By 1904 the men were business partners: Royce built the cars; Rolls sold them in London. Owners raved about their car's performance.

The partnership balanced the reserve of Royce with the exuberance of Rolls, the theory of Royce with the pragmatism of Rolls. Rolls eventually won out, and the company began building bigger, faster, more stylish cars. By 1907 the company released what would become a classic—the Silver Ghost, named for its gray color and an engine so free of noise that it ran "like a ghost."[15]

The Rolls-Royce nameplate became the epitome of luxury and performance. Neither Rolls nor Royce could have made the dream solo. But together, they laughed all the way to the bank.

On the continent another man dreamed of a new design for automobiles. Emil Jellinek dared suggest that the motor be placed in front of the driver rather than under or behind him. His prototype, which he named after his daughter, Mercedes, revolutionized automobiles but dealt a severe blow to the fortunes of a company owned by Karl Benz, who refused to adapt to change and innovation. In 1903, Benz resigned from his financially troubled company. Two decades later a new partnership formed to release the car that is now the Mercedes-Benz.[16]

To borrow a phrase from professional wrestling, you may need to *tag team* your dream. But how do you find a partner who is compatible? How long can you wait? How do you know a partner won't betray you and your dream?

Around the turn of the century a Chicago wallpaper store clerk devised a process to eliminate the need to lick stamps for envelopes. His machine would "stamp" envelopes and packages. The U.S. Post Office rejected the invention. For sixteen years Arthur Pitney searched for a way to convince the postal service of the merits of his invention. Think of the time and tongues it would save, he argued. Pitney was teased mercilessly: "Licked your problem, yet?"

However, the break came when he teamed up with a Connecticut businessman, Walter Bowes, who "sold" the post office. By 1929 Pitney-Bowes was on its way to making a difference in the mailing process.[17] Partnerships do make a difference.

I dreamed of making a film series on singleness, and I had some inkling of the enormous cost of a well-done series. I didn't want to imitate the popular Focus on the Family series or other "talking head" films (where you see the speaker and scattered shots of the audience). To illustrate my points, I wanted dramatic and comedy vignettes, which escalated production costs enormously.

I remember my first conversation with a young producer in Boston. Where would we get the money we needed to finance our dream? (If I had known then how much it would eventually cost, I never would have pursued the idea. Ah, the mystery element in the dream!) I still remember my first lunch in an airport with a financier. I gulped when he announced how much he was prepared to invest.

My task was to write the script. Others went to work to organize a limited partnership to raise the capital and to split the risk. Soon, a group of investors, many of whom I had never met, had written checks and bought into the project. In June 1983 I found myself with a troop of actors filming before a live audience in Pasadena, California.

But that isn't the end of the story. A year later, in Honolulu, the International Christian Film Distributors Association met for their version of the Academy Awards. Three film series were nominated for Best Film Series, two of which featured well-known Christian celebrities and were big-budget productions and promotions. I was just glad my series, *One Is a Whole Number,* was nominated.

I remember the phone call. I had paced my house, pondering the outcome. Frankly, second place was acceptable to me. "You beat so-and-so," the executive producer said.

"Yes, but there were three nominees," I shot back.

"_____ [he named the other celebrity] finished *second*."

The thought hit me suddenly: *We won!*

"You mean . . . we won!"

"We won."

"We" was not me but a dedicated group of producers, directors, actors, and financial investors. If no one in the Christian world had heard of Victory Films, they soon had.

Today, my award sits on my living-room mantel as a constant reminder to me of the benefits of partnering a dream. A partnership made a dream reality. And the boundaries of the dream have expanded. Each year thousands of adults, single and married, see the four films in large churches, small churches, urban churches, and country churches.

Your dream may need a partner. Be open to the possibility.

### STEP 5: LISTEN TO DREAM SHAPERS

"I can do it myself," shouts the small child, resisting, if not rejecting, a parent's offered assistance. We may laugh at such children, especially those of us who aren't parents, but that attitude is not as amusing among adults. The song "I Did It My Way" has made Frank Sinatra a lot of money because it so well represents our society. It's the *modus operandi* for a lot of dreamers, but insisting on doing it *your way* may keep the dream from ever becoming reality.

Few of our dreams end up in the original box. They need fine tuning, an occasional midcourse correction. Most of us need, from time to time, the help of dream shapers.

Christie Hauck, a former Vanderbilt University football player, quit his lucrative job as a property manager for Jacques-Miller in Nashville, Tennessee, to open a downtown cookie shop. The early components of his dream included his working at a Dairy Queen as a teenager. Later, when Christie moved back to Nashville after a few years away, he had to do something to make friends. So he made and gave away his cookies.

People began to make suggestions. A little more of this, a little less of that. A few teased, "You're in the wrong business. You ought to be making cookies for a living."

Christie had once dreamed of going to medical school. Now he dreamed of rows of perfect cookies coming out of his ovens. A few people suggested that such dreams were a tragic waste of his Vanderbilt education.

Still, he dreamed of the perfect chocolate chip cookie (hardly an original dream, for so had Debbie Fields of Mrs. Fields' Cookies fame and Wally Amos of Famous Amos Cookies). Christie flew to California and toured the Ghirardelli chocolate factory in San Francisco. He often dashed into cookie shops with a camera and snapped pictures, and he actually rummaged through the garbage of a Mrs. Fields' Cookie shop, looking for hints or clues.

Christie's friends asked for a few dozen cookies from time to time. Then he encountered Dream Shaper One: his girlfriend, Melissa Glasgow. She convinced her employer to order one hundred pounds of cookies for Christmas gifts.

But a little computation discouraged Christie. To fill that order he would have to bake cookies twenty-four hours a day, for five days, in his little apartment oven.

Now he encountered Dream Shaper Two, a friend who managed a commissary for a large restaurant in Nashville. He offered to "lend" Hauck his commercial mixers and ovens, after hours. Hauck weighed the risk.

He went for it. The thrill of seeing *his* cookies come out of *their* ovens was an incredible high for the young cookie maker. And those cookies won enthusiastic praise and requests for *more*.

Hauck approached a large department store chain in Nashville, Castner Knott, about selling his cookies in their stores. No, they responded.

Then they rethought and counteroffered. They would buy

his cookie dough and bake cookies in one of their mall stores in a Nashville suburb as an experiment. Hauck soon realized that the space they had designated was a bad location, out of the way, next to a beauty salon.

But he agreed to help out the first day of the experiment. At midmorning he was interrupted by a woman in a beautician's smock, half her hair in curlers. "Can't stand it any longer," she said breathlessly. "I've got to have some cookies!" Soon many other people began to follow their noses through the mall to Christie's Cookies.

Next, the huge Opryland, USA theme park ordered dough; mail orders began coming in. The sweet smell of success complemented the sweet smell of his cookies.

When an accountant named Laverne English ate one cookie, she volunteered to become Dream Shaper Three. Hauck would need money to expand his business, so English bought 25 percent interest in the cookie business.

Meanwhile, Christie Hauck still managed real estate in Nashville, even though some people advised him to go full-time in cookies. I mean a Vandy man couldn't have a career in cookies and be respectable. (Man cannot live by cookie dough alone!) But when the promotion with the real estate firm that he had long expected went to someone else, Hauck said yes to the dream. He leased a downtown location near the state capitol, bought $3,000 in mixers, racks, and essentials for a bakery and dived full-time into his dream.

The first morning in the new location was not as promising as Christie had hoped. His first customer walked in soon after he unlocked the door, as if on cue.

"How much is a cookie?"

When Christie told her, the would-be customer looked at Christie as if he were insane. "You won't last a week!" she declared and left.

But others bought the cookies and told their friends. In its first year, Christie Cookie Company sold 1.5 million cookies and stashed $400,000 in its corporate cookie jar. Christie shipped cookies to forty-nine states and as far away as the Persian Gulf. Soon cookie munchers were asking about franchises.

Christie Hauck could have been successful in the property management field; he could have found another promotion or another firm to hire him. Or he might have made it working for one of his cookie competitors, like Mrs. Fields or Famous Amos. But he feels that one of his greatest achievements was watching that first dream buster, who had predicted failure, come back, apologize, and buy cookies.[18]

It is not always easy to sit in a banker's or accountant's or management consultant's office and disclose your dream. They have a way of asking questions that produce instant sweat on your forehead. They have that I've-heard-it-all-before look on their faces that makes it hard for a dreamer to keeping talking. Yet many offer good suggestions—a change here, a change there, which might expedite the dream's progress.

At other times their advice must be rejected, I hope with tact. Some attach strings to their advice or assistance, to the use of their resources. Such may make your task as a dreamer far more complex. You may find yourself asking, "Is this still *my* dream?"

But you will need resources to make your dream a reality. Launching your dream requires daring

- to pursue
- to evaluate your resources
- to face your barriers
- to mortgage
- to borrow
- to be open to partnerships
- to listen to dream shapers

More importantly for success is the task of balancing these volatile elements, constructively and creatively. That could take your dream out of cold storage and onto the front line of reality.

1. Am I ready to launch my dream?

2. What are three things I would have to do immediately to launch the dream?

3. Do I need to mortgage to pursue my dreams?

4. What resources can I mortgage?

5. Do I need to borrow?

6. If yes, how much?

7. Do I have family or friends who could financially help to launch this dream?

8. How important is timing to my dream?

   _____ Very important
   _____ Somewhat important
   _____ Unimportant

   Why?

9. Should I wait for someone else to take the lead?

10. My initial response to the author's ideas about partnership is:

11. Have I thoroughly explored the potential of partnering my dream?

12. What or whom will I have to ignore in order to launch my dream?

# 6

# COMMUNICATE YOUR DREAM TO OTHERS

*Dreams are among the world's most fragile resources.* By the time people begin to put their dreams into words, they are obviously aware that dreams get destroyed in a variety of ways. Jesus illustrated this point by telling the story of the distribution of talents: One got ten, one got five, and one man got one. The first two men worked hard to use their talents productively. The man with one talent chose to bury his, fearful of losing it.

When the master demanded an account, his wrath burned against the last man because he had wasted his talent.

If only that man had had someone with whom he could have shared his dream and his fears and his wonderings about the dream, someone who would have understood. If he had, would he have hidden his dream? Probably not. After years of practice as a Swiss psychiatrist, Paul Tournier observed that self-expression is the road to self-liberation.

Your dream deserves to be heard.

However, what modern man has an overabundance of listeners? Tournier explained why so many people came to him for help. They came "to find a quiet, peaceful person who knows how to listen and who isn't thinking all the time about what he has to do next." How many dreamers long to have someone to whom they can carry their dreams, who will listen to the majesty and mystery of the dream?

"I have heard many . . . say with a sigh and a wonderful sigh, after a difficult confession, 'What a relief it is to be able to say it all at last!'" Tournier found the word *all* of great interest. *All* includes more than those things of which we are ashamed, that we fear someone will discover. *All* includes the experiences, memories, fears, dreams that frighten us, that take away our breaths, that leave us staring into space, oblivious to time. *All* includes those portions of the dream we dare not tell anyone.[1]

Martin Luther King, Jr., on a hot summer day on the steps of the Lincoln Memorial, shared his dream of a racially unprejudiced society. He elegantly declared:

> I have a dream that one day on the red hills of Georgia, the sons of former slaves and the sons of former slaveowners will be able to sit down at the table of brotherhood.
>
> I have a dream that my four little children will one day live in a nation where they will not be judged by the color of their skin, but by the content of their character.[2]

Those words on August 28, 1963, echoed like a cannon volley through the hearts of Americans. More than an eloquent string of words, more than the cadence of a gifted orator, they unveiled a heartbeat that challenged the thinking of millions of Americans. Dr. King put into words and sentences what other men only thought and felt and dreamed. And this nation worked toward making Dr. King's dream a reality because he was able to communicate it, to sell it.

On March 11, 1942, General Douglas MacArthur watched the evacuation of American forces from Corregidor, thus leaving the Philippines open to the Japanese. He sensed the anguish and fear of those who had trusted him and his army to save them from Japanese attack. He felt the agony of defeat.

MacArthur reached deep within his soul, remembering the accounts of Abraham Lincoln at the Gettysburg battlefield a century earlier. Orators had demonstrated their skills for hours that afternoon, but Lincoln stepped into history with the simple but immortal words, "Fourscore and seven years ago, our forefathers . . ." Today, no one quotes Stephen Douglas, the major speaker that afternoon. His elaborate rhetoric has been forgotten while Lincoln's simple words, the Gettysburg Address, are memorized each year by thousands of school children.

MacArthur, a student of history, wanted words that would not be lost in translation from English into the many Filipino dialects. He wanted words of promise that could be memorized by the people he was leaving.

*"I shall return."* Three words fueled the dreams and hopes of the Filipinos as they endured Japanese occupation.

Two and one-half years passed. Then, on October 20, 1944, MacArthur waded ashore at Leyte. He declared, "I *have* returned!"

MacArthur could have kept those words to himself; after all, when he said, "I shall return," there was little strong evidence to indicate that he would. Nonetheless, some days MacArthur's promise was all that kept the Filipino resistance going. He had dared to share his dream with them.[3]

Before you take this giant step, you need to evaluate your decision by asking yourself some questions, which are similar to the why? what? who? when? where? how? questions any newspaper reporter asks as he collects information for a story.

## ASK: WHY DO I TELL?

What are the principal benefits of revealing your dream?

*Conciseness.* Putting the dream into words or attempting to put it into words is a big step toward reality.

*Inching.* Dr. Robert H. Schuller is known for his observation, "Inch by inch, anything's a cinch." Inching requires the dreamer to question daily, *What have I done today to move toward my goal?* Inches add up to feet, and feet add up to yards, and yards add up to miles. You can't work toward a goal that you have not fully defined.

*Attracting a mentor.* There are individuals who will want to buy into your dream and who can offer encouragement when the going gets tough. They may have resources or contacts with resources that can bring you a step closer to reality. But they may not be mind readers who know your dream without your disclosure.

Dream spreaders are super salesmen. They realize that they cannot do the job that needs to be done alone. They do not even want to do the job alone. They look forward to spreading the dream by enlisting volunteers. The Grimké sisters illustrate this point.

They freed their own slaves. They encouraged fellow members of the Third Presbyterian Church of South Charleston in 1829—thirty years before the Civil War—to free their slaves. But to hit the trail, selling others on following their actions, meant they had to balance personal danger with the sense that God had called them to this dream. Many people who abhorred slavery, as did the Grimkés, felt that it was immoral for a woman to speak in public, especially to a mixed audience.

Angelina retorted to those who called for her to be more "ladylike" and therefore quiet, "If we surrender the right to speak to the public this year, we must surrender the right to petition the next year and the right to write the year after and so on. What then can a woman do for the slave when she is herself under the feet of men and shamed into silence?"

The Grimkés were dismissed as old maids looking for husbands, "as abnormal creatures lusting for the degenerate pleasures of publicity and as embittered spinsters venting their frustrated emotions by public attacks on the sacred and time-honored institutions of society." Some simply labeled them "cranks" or "agitators." The sisters heard the criticism, the most acid coming from their own family and closest friends. Yet each sister concluded, "Woe is me if I do not speak out on this issue."

Not only did they speak out; they encouraged the formation of abolition societies and the publication of books and pamphlets protesting slavery. Their book *American Slavery As It Really Is* was the most powerful antislavery book until the publication of *Uncle Tom's Cabin*.

Dangerous, yes. There were never enough volunteers to protect the Grimkés. Yet they traveled on—dodging rotten tomatoes, eggs, rocks, slurs, bullets—selling the dream of the end of slavery.

They did not expect to see slavery end overnight. So they worked to enlist an army of volunteers who would not settle for the expansion of slavery and who would take their place if their enemies silenced or killed them. The battle would go on until slavery was abolished.[4]

Dream spreaders plant seeds and have the faith that someday, someway the dream will unfold. Dreamers must be endowed with persistence; they have to keep on keeping on, despite the jeers, the taunts, the loudest It-can't-be-done's.

You have a choice with your dream. You can make *my* dream into *our* dream. One Grimké sister could not have made such a difference, though she did provide a powerful example in freeing her slaves. Nevertheless, through her ability to communicate her dream, she convinced others to follow her example and to join the crusade.

Another type of supporter cheers you from the sidelines. You took inventory of some of these people in chapter 2. They become your support group. The benefit of such people has been proven by the many psychologists and ministers who have founded support groups for patients suffering from alcoholism (AA and the associate groups—Alanon for spouses, Alateen for children of alcoholics), drugs, divorce, and single parenting.

"It's not what you know, it's *who* you know that counts" is a common business principle. Today, networking is a vital ingredient in making dreams come true. When you can verbally express and sell your dream, you will find individuals who will want to buy into that dream.

When Charles Lindbergh first began to toy with his dream, he realized his own limitations: He had only $2,000 saved, in case of the crash of his mail plane or a bad season. An adventure like his solo crossing of the Atlantic would cost thousands more. Where could he get that kind of money? Businessmen.

Lindbergh determined that if he could fly nonstop to Paris, St. Louis would get a lot of publicity. But businessmen think in dollars, not simply publicity. So he decided to put together a group of investors to buy the plane. Then, when he reached Paris and won the $25,000 prize, the investors would be paid off and they would still own the plane—not a bad return on their original investment.

Next, Lindbergh began to think of St. Louis businessmen who flew or who were interested in flying. He formulated a plan of action divided into seven categories—action, advantages, results, cooperation, equipment, maps, landmarks—anticipating the businessmen's questions and objections. In selling the men he had to know the advantages that would woo them and their dollars:

(1) Revive St. Louis's interest in aviation
(2) Advertise St. Louis as an aviation city
(3) Aid in making America first in the air
(4) Promote nationwide interest in aeronautics
(5) Demonstrate perfection of modern equipment

However, it was also essential to whiff reality. Lindbergh listed for the investors only two possible results:

(1) Successful completion of his flight, thus winning the $25,000 to cover his expenses
(2) Complete failure

The latter meant going down in the Atlantic Ocean and certain death.[5] The advantages of telling your dream should far outweigh the disadvantages.

## ASK: SHOULD I TELL ALL?

"How much of my dream should I reveal?" is the first question you need to ask yourself. For example, although the young mail pilot named Charles Lindbergh told a lot of people about his dream to fly across the Atlantic, *he told no one that he intended to fly solo.* His initial sales pitch to the group of St. Louis businessmen focused on what such a feat could do to promote the city as an aviation city, a city of the future. Certainly the hard-nosed businessmen had doubts: Lindbergh was too young, too inexperienced to try it; besides, did a plane capable of a trans-Atlantic flight even exist? They conceded that other people shared his dream to fly the Atlantic and claim the $25,000 Orteig Prize, but those dreamers had teams of pilots, bigger planes, and generous financial backers.[6]

Lindbergh learned that he had to balance the risk of concealing the dream and of fully, but perhaps prematurely, disclosing the dream. He learned that you cannot always reveal all the components of a dream.

### ASK: HOW DO I TELL?

Some of our dreams are like a fog, thick and not understandable. Some of our dreams defy analysis and explanation, but that's all the more reason to share them. The hearer may have clues or experiences to adequately interpret our dream or to help us move a giant step toward understanding it. I often say to people who are fumbling with their words, "Tell me the way you're thinking it." It's like a rough draft; we'll polish it later.

Also, the listener may suggest the questions that I should be asking. Those questions will be like the taps of a diamond cutter that release the gem from the uncut diamond.

### ASK: WHOM DO I TELL?

Lindbergh knew that he had to reveal his dream, but to whom? He first approached Major David Lambert, who responded, "That's quite a flight, Slim. Do you really think it can be done?" Such a question would have demolished the confidence of other men.

"Yes," Lindbergh answered, "I believe it can, but I'm going to be sure of my facts before I go much further in laying plans. That's where I need help. I want to tell the manufacturers that responsible people are behind me. If they know my backing is sound, they'll give me all the information I want about costs and performance. Otherwise, they may think it's not worthwhile spending their time."

At the end of the long conversation, Lambert offered Lindbergh $1,000. Then Lindbergh asked, "Who shall I go to next?"

"What about Major Bill Robertson, your employer?" Lindbergh carefully evaluated Robertson's stance. He would demand something more tangible than an idea. So Lindbergh perfected his plan. Robertson thoroughly quizzed the pilot on the financial details. How would he get enough money? Lindbergh used Lambert's name, which was as significant that moment to get Robertson's "Go for it" as Lambert's $1,000 check.[7]

Next, Lindbergh directly appealed to the *St. Louis Post-Dispatch*. Think of the great newspaper coverage and status they would receive for some financial support. It was a wasted appointment.

"*The Post-Dispatch* wouldn't think of taking part in such a hazardous flight. To fly across the Atlantic Ocean with one pilot and a single-engine plane. We have our reputation to consider. We couldn't possibly be associated with such a venture," the editor said curtly, dismissing Lindbergh and his dream.[8]

Dreamers need people to whom they can reveal their dream. But the question always looms, To whom? Many dreamers have gained reputations as eccentrics because they do not have enough listeners in their lives. Or because the listeners do not share the enthusiasm or technical expertise to understand the dreamer. The more scientific the dream, the fewer the pool of potential listeners.

Some of you may sense the drawbacks at this point.

Some of you have paranoid fears—whoever you tell might steal the dream.

Some of you fear rejection or ridicule.

Some of you fear a pat on the head and a "Now, now, I'm sure that everything will work out fine." Patronization.

It's one thing to have an appointment. It's another to have your listener's undivided attention, all the way to the end of the dream. It's important to be asked questions that indicate interest and move the dream forward. Lindbergh was annoyed because the editor at the *Post-Dispatch* didn't ask a single question.

Go back to Paul Tournier, who shared the manuscript for his

first book, *The Healing of Persons,* with six friends. They were thorough with their criticism, and Dr. Tournier was devastated. He assumed that their criticism meant it wouldn't make it as a book. In time he recognized the inadequacies of his manuscript. On the other hand, he wrestled with their suggestions; if he incorporated all of them, however valid, it would no longer be his book.

One friend gave him great advice: "Leave it to God."

War erupted in Europe, and Tournier found himself in the military with hours of spare time to rewrite the book.[9] Forty years later, Tournier's books have been translated into many languages and read by millions. He took a risk in sharing his dream, a manuscript. Yet he knew his critics were concerned about him and his manuscript. Had he chosen friends who had reserved or repressed their criticism, Tournier's name might today be attached to literary pabulum.

## ASK: WHEN DO I TELL?

It's essential to tell. It's necessary to have someone to tell. But when do you tell? Timing is critical.

Tournier chose to tell when he had "something in writing." Not just an abstract idea but words, sentences. I frequently teach at writer's conferences, and many would-be writers come with little more than hazy ideas. Participants who get the most out of the conferences come with written outlines and writing samples, which can be read and critiqued.

We all know people who talk a good game. They are always talking about their dreams. However, if you listen closely and ask questions, you may be surprised by the inconsistencies and the gaps.

Premature disclosure or forced disclosure is unwise. Lindbergh felt that pressure when the Wright Air Company turned him down: "We don't want to put our reliance on a single-engine plane over the ocean." Lindbergh continued to fly his mail runs through the bitterly cold winter of 1926–27, aware that he was falling farther behind the well-financed teams. Some nights his dream seemed a hopeless waste of his backers' money. There was no prize for being second to cross the Atlantic; he had to be the *first!*

Lindbergh now approached Harry Knight, a young broker and president of the St. Louis Flying Club. Lindbergh sold him on the idea of a single-engine flight and he, in turn, contacted his friend Harold Bixby at the State National Bank. Days passed before Bixby agreed. "Slim, you've sold us on this proposition of yours. It's a tough job you're taking on, but we've talked it over and we're with you. From now on you'd better leave the financial end to us."[10]

There is the reason for revealing. Had Lindbergh been forced to continue trying to raise money on his own, nickle-and-diming his way to the dream, he would not have had the time to redesign the plane to make the dream happen. Now he had a core of men with sufficient money to finance the dream.

However, still more rejection was to come. The Travel Air Company in Kansas built the plane Lindbergh knew could make the flight, so he made his appeal to them: What an opportunity for your company. Air Travel politely refused to get involved. Lindbergh was forced to pitch his dream to tiny Ryan Airlines in San Diego. Yes, they could build the plane Lindbergh wanted, but it would take at least three months.

"Three months!" Lindbergh fumed. The competition for the Orteig Prize could be lost if he waited that long. "Couldn't you build it in two months?" he pleaded.[11]

Lindbergh persuaded them.

Another company intervened and offered Lindbergh the plane he really wanted, the Wright-Bellanca, for $15,000. It was far more than Lindbergh's backers had projected, but they agreed to the price for the best plane. In New York as the final arrangements were being negotiated, Lindbergh was stunned to discover this clause in the agreement: *We reserve the right to select the crew that flies it.* At that point, Lindbergh realized the builders would never agree to a solo flight or for him to be the pilot. His euphoria evaporated.[12]

Now it had to be the Ryan plane, and he had lost precious

time. By February 23, 1927, when Lindy arrived in San Diego, Ryan had agreed to forego their profit on the plane, but Lindbergh wanted a guarantee the plane could make it to Paris. No profit, no guarantee, they countered.

So Lindbergh faced a decision. Could he risk his backers' money? He decided to discuss the question with Donald Hall, Ryan's chief engineer. "Where will you put the cockpits?" Hall asked.

"I will only need one cockpit," Lindbergh replied.

"One cockpit?" Hall blustered. "You don't plan on making that flight alone, do you?"[13]

Lindbergh recognized the criticalness of his answer. Now was the time to attract one last backer to his dream.

Lindbergh revealed his dream. Without an extra man, the *Spirit of St. Louis* could carry three hundred and fifty pounds of gasoline; it would be shorter and lighter. A solo flight would also mean that he had not endangered another man's life to fulfill his own dream.

Timing had been critical. Lindbergh already had his backers with him and the Ryan engineers behind him *before* he revealed that it had to be a solo flight. Lindbergh knew the moment to tell *all*.

It's difficult for us to comprehend the risk involved in Lindbergh's adventure in our age of the 747 jets and the Concorde that flies to Paris in a few hours. Perhaps a more contemporary example of revealing the dream would be wise.

Luis Alfredo Galarza's son was born with a cleft palate, webbed fingers, and a deformed skull that would not allow the brain to grow. Ecuadorian doctors gave the baby six months to live, at best. The medical attention the boy needed did not exist in Ecuador, and the family did not have funds to afford the care that did exist in America.

Luis had a choice: to accept the professional judgment and to mourn *or* to find a way for a miracle to happen. He began writing hospitals around the world, begging for help. The first break came through Interplast, a group of American plastic surgeons and nurses who donate vacation time to medical service in Third World nations. Luis met Dr. Richard Greminger of Fort Lauderdale when Greminger came to Ecuador through Interplast and corrected the boy's cleft palate. But Greminger advised Luis that more sophisticated cranial surgery was needed soon. That surgery was eventually performed by a surgeon from St. Louis.[14]

Three years passed. Luis, Jr., could not color with a crayon, hold a baseball bat, or catch a football because of his webbed hands. In Florida medical care to correct such deformities is readily available to children at an early age. So Dr. Greminger went to work on his many contacts. He approached Pembroke Pines General Hospital near Fort Lauderdale with a "would-you-be-willing-to?" series of questions. The hospital agreed to provide the lab work, hospital stay, and surgical expenses. Then he approached other specialists, including Dr. Gary Schwartz. An orthopedic surgeon, Schwartz had earlier indicated he would be interested in doing some hand work on a case of Greminger's choosing. Now Schwartz cleared time on his schedule.

The expense of flying the boy and his parents to the United States and their living expenses during his recovery remained a problem until the hospital administrator, Ed Moss, stepped in. He contacted the Weston Rotary Club, enlisting their help, and Dr. Greminger composed a medical team to donate the expenses. All was now in place to create a medical miracle.

On May 29, 1987, three-year-old Luis, Jr., was wheeled into an operating room at Pembroke Pines, and the surgical team, headed by Dr. Schwartz, went to work to form three fingers from skin grafts off the boy's groin and to lengthen his thumbs.

The operation was a stunning success.

The operation and expenses, which would easily have totaled $40,000, were realized because a father dreamed that his son could have a normal life. He sold his house in Ecuador to help pay a small fraction of those expenses. But Luis, Sr., said after the successful surgery, "I'd do it again a thousand times if I had to."

Why did Dr. Greminger and his friends become involved in Luis Galarza's dream? In the case of Lindbergh's backers, money and fame and a place in history books were the motivation, but involvement with Luis, Jr., cost his doctors money, since it took them from patients who could pay.

Greminger told me that he was involved for three reasons: the joy that it gave the parents; the feeling it gave him; and most importantly, the knowledge that the boy's recovery would have been impossible any other way.[15] A group of humanitarian dreamers gave a little boy the gift of a future.

There's a saying, "You have not because you ask not." That applies to dreams. Luis, Sr., refused to give up his dream. Charles Lindbergh didn't let the word *no* abort his. Neither should you.

Do yourself and the world a big favor: Speak up.

〜〜〜〜〜〜〜〜〜〜〜〜〜

1. What keeps me from telling all?

2. Are there parts of my dream that need to be kept hidden?

3. What are those parts?

4. When will I disclose those?

5. How do I tell? Write out your dreams completely. Think of this as a rough draft.

6. Whom do I tell? Who are the people whose input is necessary to make the dream come true?

7. In what order should parts of the dream be told?

8. Whom should I not tell about my dream?

9. When do I tell?

10. Why do I tell? What do I gain?

# 7

## STEP SIX

# HAVE FAITH IN YOURSELF AND THE DREAM

In an age when almost anyone can hum, "I did it *my* way," when restaurants say, "Have it *your* way," some people try to solo a dream.

Dreams require a partnership, investing all of yourself into the dream with God's participation. Our culture praises and values individualism because it took a degree of rugged individualism to pull up roots in Europe to come to the New World. But too many are forever denied the promised land because of their insistence, "I can do it myself."

Two thousand years ago, the author of Hebrews said, "Now faith is the substance of things hoped for, the evidence of things not seen."[1] The J. B. Phillips translation of the Bible makes it stronger: "It means being certain of things we cannot see."[2]

On a clear day you can see forever, but on some days, even clear ones, others cannot see the dream you point to. Despite your "Don't you see's?" they look at you blankly. What keeps the dreamer looking toward the horizon? What is it that summons a dreamer from a night's sleep with expectancy, while others fear only a day like so many others? What is it that causes a dreamer, after repeated failures, to try again?

Faith.

My life was revolutionized through reading a book while on a beach vacation. It was not light pop reading, but contained words that leaped off the page and challenged my mind to question. The words provoked an intense internal struggle about who am I? why am I here? why at this particular time? where have I come from? and, more importantly, where am I headed?

In *Exploring Spiritual Direction,* Alan Jones asked three questions:

1. Do I really believe that my life comes to me as a gift and that there is in me a terrific thing?
2. Am I, in the middle of my own struggles, daring enough to ask for help, seek guidance, cultivate friendships?
3. Am I sincere in wanting to respond to my longing for God, especially when I know and fear the revolutionary changes that may be involved?[3]

I copied those three questions into my journal and added one word: *Well?*

## DREAMERS BELIEVE

I believe that in the moment we first breathe, God dreams a dream for every one of us, and everytime God thinks of us, he remembers our dream. If some days it seems as if God is crowding us, it is because he is so anxious to see us complete our dream.

Dreamers realize that God is the source of their dream if it is noble and worthy. Therefore, it is easy for dreamers to recognize that a Higher Power is at work. What many would call coincidence, dreamers know to be the working of God. No wonder they won't take no for an answer.

As a dreamer, I rely on two passages of Scripture: Genesis 1, from the Old Testament, and Hebrews 11, from the New Testament. "In the beginning God created . . ." Created what? "The heavens and the earth."[4] This is the stage upon which all great dreams will be played.

Then I read, "The earth was without form, and void; and

darkness was on the face of the deep," until God said, "Let there be . . . *and there was*."[5]

God the Creator is still creating dreams through people. Many of the things we enjoy God could have given and created. Adam and Eve could have had computers (though I'm not sure who would have serviced them). Rather, God chose to plant seeds in the minds of human beings, then to sit back and watch it all unfold.

To this day, when God wants something done, he rarely raises an army. He plants an idea into a dreamer and waits.

I can't prove it, but I believe that on occasion, God has stopped the music of heaven to listen to a small child say, "When I get big, I'm going to . . ." Otherwise, why would he have sent His Son as a baby? But I also have to believe that God works continually to rekindle the dream, to call us back to the dream, when defeat, rebellion, discouragement have obscured it.

## BY FAITH

The eleventh chapter of Hebrews is considered by many to be one of the greatest chapters in the Bible. It's like walking through a museum with a host who explains the portraits hanging on the wall:

"*By faith* Abel offered to God . . .

"*By faith* Noah . . . prepared an ark . . .

"*By faith* Abraham . . . went out . . .

"*By faith* Sarah . . . bore a child . . .

"*By faith* Moses . . . forsook Egypt . . .

"*By faith* the harlot Rahab did not perish . . . ."[6]

Those words resound like timpani in an orchestra. But they do not end in Scripture; they continue to this day. *By faith*, Harold Ivan Smith . . . And someday that blank will be filled in, if, by faith, I complete the dream.

An old gospel song says, "By faith, I received my sight." That's true of the individuals in this book. They saw something that no one else could see; they heard something that no one else could hear; they longed for something that no one else could achieve. By faith they accomplished their dreams.

By faith you can accomplish your dream. *By faith*. There are no asterisks noting, "Except for the following . . ."

The author of Hebrews recognized several great dreamers, yet one is predominant—Abraham. Abraham had a problem. He had no son. The culture demanded an heir. Abraham had lived with the problem until he was almost one hundred years old. Then God promised him that a "son *coming from your body* will be your heir."[7] I doubt that Abraham had taken Health and Hygiene 101, and this was centuries before Sex Education, but Abraham knew reality. A son was a biological impossibility—at least, with his current wife, who was ninety years old.

God chose to use visual aids. He took Abraham out into the star-spangled night and said, "Look up. Count the stars." Abraham must have laughed at that impossible task. Then God concluded, "So shall your offspring be."[8]

God didn't just inform Abraham once. Again, he reminded Abraham of the promise, an heir *through Sarah*. This time, Abraham fell down laughing, mumbling, "Will a son be born to a man a hundred years old?"

Apparently, his laughter was contagious. Sarah also laughed, calling herself "worn out." The Lord confronted Abraham about his wife's attitude: "Why did Sarah laugh?" Then the Lord demanded of Abraham, "Is anything too hard for the LORD?"[9]

That question comes to you as well. If you have faith, is anything too hard for the God who dreams *with* us?

Centuries later, a descendant of Abraham wrote, "And so from this one man, and he as good as dead, came descendants as numerous as the stars in the sky and as countless as the sand of the seashore."[10]

Some onlookers might consider you "as good as dead" as far as your capacities to launch and complete the dream. Instead, say, "Dream on." Fortunately, Abraham's dream happened in a day before governmental paperwork. Can you imagine what would happen in the Social Security offices if they had to process papers for a baby's birth to a ninety-year-old woman? How much would the *National Enquirer* pay for that story? But Abraham perceived the dream as an opportunity rather than as a problem.

What about you? How are you faithing your dream? What about those troublesome times when your cheerleaders are silent, when the fog of discouragement swirls around you? If you are going to achieve your dream and if your dream stimulates the dreams of others, you will have to cash in all your Lone Ranger fantasies. Your dream needs—and if it is noble, merits—faith.

## 1. Faith Encourages the Dreamer

In the field of civil rights, the beaches and lunch counters and bus station restrooms and schools would still be segregated had blacks bought into the Lone Ranger concept. In fact, their success in challenging racism and bigotry may be attributed to the fact that most of their leaders were clergy and most of their campaign rallies were held in churches. Their heroes were biblical heroes. Their faith nourished their dreamseeds; their faith would not accommodate the voices that urged them to "leave things be."

White children in Florida took it for granted that beaches were there to be used. Black children did not have such a luxury. The better beaches were for "Whites Only." The dream to be able to swim in the Atlantic was stirred up by every child's question, "Why can't *we* swim there?" Every parent's answer seemed shallow. The human spirit rejected "because" and whispered "someday!"

Such questions and the long-delayed promises troubled Edward T. Graham. He wasn't content to organize a chapter of the NAACP or National Urban League or to pastor the Zion Baptist Church in Miami. The Reverend Graham had to do something about the dream. He could have preached forever but the Whites Only signs would never have come down. So he organized a nonviolent wade-in to protest the discrimination that kept blacks off beaches in Miami. If people drove or flew a thousand miles to swim here, why couldn't black children ride a few blocks to swim on a hot day? he asked.

Voices challenged Graham's leadership. "Whites won't like that." Or "We might get beaten and arrested." Or worse.

Graham reminded his congregation, "It is far better to die a thousand deaths standing on our feet than to live a million years on our bellies." That was not just good preaching but the creed by which Graham chose to live.[11]

Today Miami's beaches are open to all.

## 2. Faith Helps Dreamers Challenge Circumstances

Earlier I stated that dreams come in particular settings and times. I have also said that we live in an it-can't-be-done world. Verbalize your dream and hardly before your words are out, someone is telling you why it can't be done. Or why it can't be done *here*. Or why it can't be done *now*.

Shirley Finn, coordinator of the baccalaureate nursing program at the University of Texas at Arlington, illustrated this principle. As a child, Shirley had dreamed of being a nurse. As a young, black North Carolinean, she launched her dream by scrubbing floors on her hands and knees to make enough money to attend Saint Augustine College in Raleigh. In 1955 she received her degree in nursing and got a job as a nurse in Elizabeth City, making $87 a month. After searching for a better-paying position, she was hired by a suburban hospital near Chicago. Even there she found discrimination, yet she would not fast-forward her dream.

That dream took a giant step when a noted surgeon chose her to be his scrub nurse, an incredible honor. "To a black nurse," Shirley Finn said, "it was a miracle." People who have faith see miracles where others see coincidences.

Eventually she moved on to teach nursing in Greensboro, North Carolina, just as the civil rights movement took on full swing. "It was a time when change had to be made; when the

'Blacks Only' signs had to come down, and the 'back-of-the-bus' time had to come to an end."[12]

When Finn married and moved to Texarkana, Texas, her accomplishments were wiped out. Shirley had to start over as the hospital's first black nurse and daily dealt with aloofness or outright rejection.

Shirley kept her mind on her dream. "It was painful, living through that, but there are some things more important than the pain—serving your God, for example, and helping others professionally." Time and patience worked in her favor as she challenged her circumstances. In 1966 she became the first black nursing instructor at Texarkana Community College; by 1971 she was the head of the associate nursing program. She now serves as chairman of the Health Occupations Division, as well as coordinator of the transfers to the University of Texas.[13]

Whatever the arena of your dream, you will need patience to make that dream a reality and patience to challenge the circumstances.

### 3. Faith Helps the Dreamer Pace the Quest

In school most of us learned the tale of the hare and the tortoise and their famous race. The writer of Ecclesiastes observed, "The race is not to the swift or the battle to the strong . . . but time and chance happen to them all."[14]

I grew up near Churchill Downs, home of the Kentucky Derby. One thing I learned is that horse races are seldom won by the first horse out of the starting gate. In 1986 Ferdinand, ridden by Willie Shoemaker, stunned everyone by coming from last place to a spectacular finish that brought fans out of their seats screaming, "Didya see that? Incredible!"

Henry David Thoreau said, "If a man [dreamer] does not keep pace with his companions, perhaps it is because he hears a different drummer. Let him step to the music which he hears, however measured or far away."[15]

Some dreamers blaze a trail; others take their own time. They're called late bloomers. A careful reading of the history of the arts and other fields documents fast-laners or bright young lights who burned out early and the story of the eventual triumph of the late bloomers.

In 1980 an unknown electrician working in the Gdansk shipyards called himself a "delinquent worshiper." Lech Walensa continued, "I pondered upon God's existence and looked for signs to confirm Him, but faith did not grow in me until life grew harder. The more difficult my path became, the closer I came to the faith."[16]

A priest had sternly warned him in his youth that if he did not change his ways he would spend his life in prison. No one would have chosen him as a person who would make a difference.

"I was incapable of saying anything in public. My tongue used to outrun my mind. I was unable to keep track of the words I said. I would always speak before I thought and was therefore a poor public speaker." But he had a brain and he had friendships with hundreds of other workers. And he had a conviction that the Communist government of Poland was corrupt. He dreamed of a time when workers could unite and do something about the injustice.

In August 1981 Lech Walensa stepped forward and founded the Solidarity labor union and set in motion an inevitable confrontation with the Polish government that gained the attention of the world. Soon he found himself followed by secret police. Eventually he was confined to his home as the authorities attempted to break the power of Solidarity. Walensa maintained that he did not sign a contract with the Lord but that something happened in August when he began to speak, in rough, grammatically incorrect Polish. When he spoke, Poles listened (as did leaders in Rome, Moscow, and Washington, D.C.). Overnight he became a symbol of courage.

> I am convinced that my faith had a powerful impact upon me during the time of my confinement. . . . God, our Lord, distinguishes each one of us from all the others; he assigned a task for every person. . . . I simply believe in Providence. I believe that I am here to execute the verdicts of Providence. This is

precisely why I can accomplish significantly more than if I were just Lech Walensa, without God directing my fate. It's good to have the awareness of that great force outside us and above us directing our lives.[17]

Lech Walensa found his hope and courage deeply rooted in his faith. When he was awarded the Nobel Peace Prize in 1981, he was not allowed to go to Oslo to receive it. His absence became an indictment of the Communist regime. How is it possible that a mere shipyard worker could become the confidante of the pope or *Time*'s Man of the Year? I would answer "by faith." But wasn't he afraid? Walensa himself answered, "Deep religious belief, deep faith, eliminates fear."[18]

You may not be facing a Communist regime. But you may be facing what seem to be insurmountable obstacles. Faith finds a way through the circumstances if the dreamer paces the dream.

Premature acquisition of the dream has devastated some impatient dreamers. There is something about the maturing that occurs, the additional skills a dreamer assumes and develops, during the pacing that enhances the eventual attainment of the dream. Walensa has admitted that he and the underground members of Solidarity are still learning. And the last word has not been yet been written on the movement.

Pacing insures a dream apprenticeship, a time to try on the dream.

## 4. Faith Gives the Dreamer Courage to Ask for Help

Barbara Sher and Annie Gottlieb in *Wishcraft: How to Get What You Really Want Out of Life,* noted, "Mankind wanted the moon for thousands of years, and in the twentieth century we got there. That's what wishing *plus* technique can do: it can change reality."[19] But wishing won't make it happen.

Priorities are the roadmaps for getting from point A to point B. The dreamer has to know when and how to ask for help to bridge the points.

Mary McLeod Bethune may have been one of the nation's best askers. She was born the fifteenth of seventeen children to

South Carolina sharecroppers. Her father prayed that God would show him which child to send to school. He chose Mary. She went from the cotton fields to a little mission school operated by the Presbyterian Church, on to Scotia College, and eventually to Moody Bible Institute in Chicago. She wanted to go to Africa as a missionary but was told the doors were closed to blacks.

So she taught school, hoping that the mission board might change its mind. She called the period of waiting "cruel days."

Five years passed. From a traveling Methodist minister, Mary learned of the desperate conditions for blacks around Daytona, Florida, where many had moved to work on the railroad. They needed help. With one dollar and fifty cents, Mary and her son, Albert, then five years old, headed for Daytona to open a school for black girls. "Do we have enough money for a school?" her son asked. Mary looked at her purse and answered, "That's all we have, so I guess it will have to do."

On an abandoned garbage dump called "Hell's Hole," Mrs. Bethune launched her dream—a school for blacks. Although the owner wanted a thousand dollars for the property, Mary offered two hundred—five dollars down and five dollars a month.[20]

Many white citizens opposed the school, asking, "Why do black children, especially females, need an education?" "Because," Mary answered. By 1911 she had opened a school for blacks. Her students sat on benches made out of dry goods boxes; they slept on mattresses stuffed with moss. Some mornings they fished, then fried the fish, made sandwiches, and sold them to railroad workers. Then they had afternoon classes.

Mary Bethune possessed a dream that someday black women would stand with their heads held high. She knew that her dream required boldness, sacrifice, and constant interpretation to skeptics.

Part of her dream hinged on her willingness to beg. The nearby Daytona Beach community attracted many wealthy northerners who owned winter homes. Mary approached Robert Gamble (of Proctor and Gamble) and asked him to visit the Hell's Hole campus, which was little more than a log cabin and five students.

"I want you to be a trustee," she said.

"Of what?" Gamble asked, looking around.

"Of the thing that I have in my head to do."

After listening to her dream, Proctor said yes.

Later, Mary Bethune said:

> I am always building spiritual air castles. Only those with spiritual understandings can appreciate my feelings when I say that I saw in my mind's eye the Bethune-Cookman College of today—even in that first week in 1904, when I was surrounded by little children sitting on dry goods boxes with questioning faces turned to me.[21]

No wonder she named the first major building, Faith Hall. With Gamble's encouragement (he was a trustee for twenty years), Mary buttonholed other winter visitors, such as Theodore Roosevelt. She held open house on Sunday afternoons and invited guests to come to see the dream. And she could do wonders with five minutes of a visitor's time.

Mrs. Bethune had a beautiful voice and organized a singing ensemble, which serenaded visitors of the seaside hotels. John D. Rockefeller became a friend and benefactor after hearing one of her groups sing. She often sang the spiritual "Keep in the Middle of the Road": "Don't you turn to the right, don't you turn to the left. Keep in the middle of the road." That spiritual expressed Mary's strategy for underwriting her dream.

Her close friend Booker T. Washington had given her invaluable advice on the process of asking. He took Mary's hands and illustrated his point: "When you go out to ask for help, go out with the open hand. If you fist up your hand, you are neither ready to give nor to receive. With the open hand, you are ready to give *and* to receive."[22]

What kept her asking or, as some would have labeled it, begging? To have blacks as part of the great family of mankind was her ultimate goal, and the college was a vehicle to prepare them for the future.

Her estranged husband, just before his death in 1919, demanded, "Why? Why are you doing this? Doesn't your happiness, the happiness of your family mean anything? Don't you ever get tired of trying to hold this school together?"

She answered, "It will be worth it. When the girls can receive a good education, grow up healthy and strong. This is my life's work."

How did she ask so effectively, once getting $10,000 from Marshall Field in less than ten minutes? "I had faith in God; faith in my people and in my friends; and faith in Mary McLeod Bethune."[23]

Today in Daytona, Bethune-Cookman College, a coed liberal arts college, with thousands of distinguished graduates, is a lasting legacy to a dreamer who knew how to ask.

## 5. Faith Helps the Dreamer See Opportunity in Every Problem or Catastrophe

I love the opening line of the national anthem, *"Oh, say can you see?"* The question, when Francis Scott Key wrote the song, was asking if he could see the flag of the infant nation flying, over Fort McHenry near Baltimore.

I paraphrase that question for dreamers, *"Can you see the dream?"* Like the fog Edison described, some have to rely on faith for vision. I have driven through some thick fogs, relying only on the white lines on the side of the road for direction. What a relief to have the fog lift and to be able to resume my speed.

Not all dreams are seen in bright sunshine. Sometimes it is in the agony of defeat that a dream is launched. How do you see the inevitable obstacles: as problems or as opportunities? Your perspective may well determine the outcome.

On August 21, 1983, Benigno Aquino called his wife before he boarded a plane that would take him home to Manila. After years in exile, he was returning to the Philippines to do political battle with his old adversary, Ferdinand Marcos. When Marcos

had declared martial law in 1972, the first man he jailed was
Aquino, charging him with murder, subversion, and illegal pos-
session of firearms.

For seven and one-half years he languished in prison, nursing
his bitterness and resentment. The guards let dogs eat half his
dinner and then gave him what was left. His only link to the
outside world was his wife, who faithfully visited him in spite
of the embarrassing strip searches she had to endure.

In 1980, under pressure from President Jimmy Carter,
Marcos released Aquino to come to the United States for triple
bypass heart surgery. He accepted academic posts at Harvard
and M.I.T. Life was good in exile. But he dreamed of returning
to the Philippines, either to serve in the government or to serve
out his prison sentence. His wife waited, too, content as a
homemaker. Then President Marcos, still under pressure from
Carter, called for snap parliamentary elections. Benigno recognized his opportunity to go home and prepare the opposition
for those elections.[24]

Within hours, before stunned reporters, Aquino was gunned
down as he disembarked from the plane. Suddenly, Corazon
Aquino, a young mother of five, became a widow and at the
same time a victim. Only two months before, she had registered
to vote and had listed "housewife" as her occupation on her
application. The last office she had held was valedictorian of
her sixth grade class.

Her husband's supporters suggested that she run for the presidency. "No," she protested. But slowly she began to see the
opportunity of a democratic government in the Philippines.
The only candidate who could defeat Marcos would be someone who was his total opposite—naive, innocent, a person of
faith. Marcos laughed at having such an easy opponent and
lewdly suggested that a woman's place was in the bedroom.[25]

He didn't count on the tenacity of the small woman behind
the big glasses, who always wore yellow. Suddenly, she offered
what millions of Filipinos wanted, innocence and a cause—to
complete her husband's dream.

The outcome seemed predetermined; it was just a question

of what Marcos's winning margin would be, because he wrote the rules and had henchmen to carry them out. Marcos had the army and the wealthy businessmen. Aquino had only faith to offer to millions of peasants.

Cory had a dream and she was able to sell her dream to the people. She had a strong faith that motivated the dream. That faith had sustained her when she led millions of people through the streets for her husband's funeral. That faith led her to spiritual leaders such as Jaime Cardinal Sin. That faith led her to prayer before her decisions. Those who know her say that prayer is an important part of her daily life and decision making. She counsels with advisors and trusted friends; then she seeks divine guidance.

Sandra Burton has observed, "Although waiting for inspiration may slow her down, it also produces resolute action once she makes up her mind." She wrestled with the decision to run for president; she believed that she had "exhausted the advice of others without finding an answer." She entered a church and "'prayed as I had never prayed before,' saying, 'Please, Lord, tell me what to do.'"[26]

Finally she realized she had to get away from everyone. In a convent outside Manila, she spent an entire day in prayer, seeking God's direction. The next day she announced her decision: she would run.

Slowly, the impossible began to unfold. Marcos panicked. "Marcos's men ripped up ballots, bought others and intimidated voters at gunpoint. As many as three million names were simply struck off the voter lists."[27]

Thousands of poll watchers and volunteers took part in the dream. They sang hymns and burned candles as they formed a human barricade against Marcos's armed thugs. With heads high and hearts pounding, they carried their ballot boxes through the streets to the counting stations. Nuns faced down the goons; mothers disarmed soldiers.

Then on February 14, the National Assembly announced, to no one's surprise but to the world's consternation, that Marcos had been reelected. The dream had been defeated. Business continued as usual in the Philippines until one million people took to the streets and converged on Luneta Park in downtown Manila. The cries of "Cory, Cory" echoed through the city. Marcos's troops were on full alert and were prepared to crush the protesters.

The writer Charles Colson said, "This was the kind of crowd a politician might dream of. They would march anywhere, do anything, on command."[28] Marcos had played his hand; the next move was Cory's.

Cory could have pointed in the direction of Marcos's Malacalang Palace, and the people would have stampeded toward it. But because of her faith, she made a simple request; she asked them to pray. Soon Ferdinand Marcos was receiving his mail in exile.

Later, when reporters asked her if she believed God had a plan for her, Cory responded, "God has a plan for all of us, and it is for each of us to find out what that plan is. I can tell you that I never thought the plan was for me to be president."[29]

Didn't she realize that the same persons who ordered her husband's assassination could kill her? "If someone wishes to use a bazooka on me, it's good-bye. If it's my time to die, I'll go."[30]

Chuck Colson reported his meeting with her on the eve of her departure for a state visit to Japan, which many feared would produce a coup. Some predicted the defiant defense minister, Juan Enrile, would be president within hours.

Cory Aquino was relaxed. Why? "I didn't seek this," she informed Colson, "and I only want to serve my people. I simply have to put my trust in the Lord."[31]

Mrs. Aquino's dream succeeded against incredible odds. She has not had an easy time. She has put down coups by disgruntled army officers; she has battled with investors pulling out of the Philippines. Still, her faith encourages Cory to dream.

## CONCLUSION

Faithing the dream is a big step toward reality. But faith is essential to completing the dream. You can only go so far up the ladder toward your dream on your own, in your own strength.

The placement of this chapter at this point in the book is not coincidental. You will go no further without a stockpile of faith. No wonder Cory Aquino, two months after taking office, could say to the governors of the Asian Development Bank, "I am not embarrassed to tell you that I believe in miracles."[32]

You see, by faith, Cory Aquino had the courage to return to the Philippines. By faith Cory had the courage to run for president. And by faith she has had the stamina to stay in office. One hundred years from today, someone will look back to her leadership and see her faith blazing like a diamond in the sunlight.

God dreams dreams for his children and uses those dreams like pieces in a jigsaw puzzle to accomplish his dream. God invites us to participate with him in dreaming. That takes faith, but what dividends it pays. Faithing makes dreams happen.

You have the potential to join the list of heroes in Hebrews 11. The author said, "And what more shall I say? For the time would fail me to tell of Gideon and Barak and Samson and Jephthah."[33] In the text there may be a period, but in reality the list goes on and on, down through the centuries, one dreamer following another.

From this vantage point, we can see how each dreamer, each man of faith, has stood on the shoulders of the previous generation. Dreams have triumphed over war, opposition, plagues, disbelief, ridicule. It is as if faith has been passed from one generation of dreamers to the next with the simple instruction, "Go."

What Tim Stafford said of scientists is true of dreamers as well:

As we look forward, scientific knowledge seems to flow smoothly, almost inevitably forward. The timing may have been delayed a few years or even decades, but sooner or later someone will make the next jump. The church may have threatened Galileo with the stake, but his clear vision triumphed, for he saw things the way they really are. Progress does not even ultimately depend on the rare genius. An Einstein speeds things up, but as long as there are real scientists practicing real science, man's knowledge must expand, his mastery increase.[34]

Thus the dreamer stands poised between the past and the future. Those whom he follows, and those who follow him, strain to see what decision he will make. No wonder the author of Hebrews said so boldly, "Therefore . . . since we are surrounded by so great a cloud of witnesses, let us lay aside every weight, and the sin which so easily ensnares us, and let us run with endurance the race that is set before us."[35]

That's what faith does. Faith helps us see the dream, embrace the dream, and focus on the race with persistence. Faith makes the difference. Otherwise, the steps up the dream stairwell will be wasted. Faith could be *the* factor that determines that your dream will become reality. Faith gives dreamers the courage to try.

~~~~~~~~~~~~~~~~~~~~~~~~

1.  Do I really believe that my life and dream are gifts?

2.  In what ways do I demonstrate that I value those gifts?

3.  Have I been willing to ask for help with my dream?

4.  It's one thing to seek guidance, as the author suggests, but another to accept and utilize it. What is my track record?

5.  In relation to my faith, what are some possible "revolutionary changes" that I fear as by-products of my dream?

6. Do I buy the author's notion, "In the moment we first breathe, God dreams a dream for every one of us, no exceptions"?

7. Is impatience one of the barriers to my dream?
   If so, why?

8. How have I sensed God's working in my dream?

9. What were my first impressions when I heard of Lech Walensa? Fool? Media-hungry? Gutsy?

10. To whom have I specifically turned for help with my dream?

11. Whom have I wanted to ask for help but have postponed asking?

# 8

# LEARN TO RESTORE
# THE DREAM

The unthinkable happened for dozens of small-business owners who leased space in a three-story office building in downtown Hayward, California. For several hours the building burned out of control, each hour destroying more dreams and businesses. Joe Oakman had had his barber shop in the building for more than thirty-two years. Others had been tenants for only a few months.

Oakman said, "It's sad to wipe out a whole life's work in just a few short hours." A Korean businessman, Gyeon Kim, said, "I will try to reopen. I don't have any insurance."

Al Adams was like Kim. "I don't have any insurance either." Adams, who had opened his photography shop a year before, having worked as a free lancer to make enough money to launch his dream of his own studio, concluded, "I'm finished. Nice to know you. There's nothing I can do now. I don't have the money to start again. It's all over unless I win the lottery."

Even for those who were insured, it was to be a long time before "business as usual." One accountant estimated that it would take years for her to reconstruct the tax records of her clients.

An antique store owner arrived just in time to see firemen directing the water into his shop, which contained 1860-vintage furniture, handmade quilts, a turn-of-the-century Edison phonograph, and other treasures collected through the years. Most of his items were uninsured because he could not insure them for their actual value and be competitive. But Bill Matteson was far more optimistic than the other tenants: "We'll go out, buy some more antiques, and open at another location near here."

The headline in the *San Francisco Chronicle* boldly declared, "Dreams Destroyed As Businesses Burn in Hayward."[1] I'm not sure the headline was accurate. The dreams will only be destroyed *if* those shop owners and merchants give in to their crisis.

Life has a way of poofing dreams. What a tornado does in the Midwest, what hurricanes do in the South along the Gulf, reality can do anywhere through a fire or a flood. In some of those moments, one senses that the destructive forces can go either way, full destruction or only partial destruction. But the dreamer must still hope, pray, and wait.

Fires also affect inventors. Thomas Alva Edison learned about their destructive impact on dreams one night in 1914. He had just left his Menlo Park, New Jersey, laboratories when a fire broke out. A messenger caught up with him at home. "Mr. Edison, come quick. The lab's on fire."

By the time Edison arrived, everything except the main lab and library was in flames. "There was nothing I could do but watch," Edison said. Many men would have been distraught but not Edison. Turning to his son Charles, he ordered, "Get mother and her friends over here. They'll never see a fire like this again." Some bystanders thought the old inventor had lost his mind.

Edison didn't go to bed that night. Instead, he told the men what machinery and merchandise to try to save. The next morning he sorted through the ruins. Naturally, his friends came to comfort him. "I told them I was only sixty-seven, not too old to make a fresh start." Yet he wondered aloud to his son, "What'll we use for money?" He had thought his buildings were fireproof, so the entire plant was underinsured.

His friend Henry Ford arrived at the scene and looked around, but didn't say much. Finally, he handed Edison a check. "You'll need some money. Let me know if you need more." Edison looked at the check: $750,000. In 1914 that was a lot of money.

Over the years, Edison paid off the loan, but Ford would never accept any interest. Ford knew what to say, when to say it, and how to say it. He helped a sixty-seven year old restore the dream. And some of Edison's great inventions came *after* the fire.[2]

Others watch a gradual deterioration of the dream. I noticed an obituary in a Kansas City paper. For a young, Nebraska-born dancer, the dream died on May 5, 1986, far from the stages in New York, where he had tapped out his dream. A killer disease, AIDS, ended his dream and the dreams of his parents. And there are a hundred diseases that attack dreams: heart attacks, diabetes, common diseases, and those that are difficult to spell and pronounce. Americans give generously each year to fund-raising campaigns to do something about those dream spoilers.

Yet for some the deterioration of a dream begins not in some body part but deep in the spirit of the dreamer. Some people no longer talk as often or as enthusiastically as they once did about *the* dream. Sadly, some dreamers sabotage their own dreams. For every dreamer like Kevin, who left a Nebraska farm to go to the Big Apple to chase his dream, ten have stayed home, afraid to try, afraid of failure.

Some dreams are fragile, like the china in one of those shops with all the Ask for Assistance signs. It's never as much fun to shop there. I'm always afraid I'll make one clumsy move, and . . .

Yet other dreams are tough. As I write this, I'm sitting on the beach in Florida, staring at a twenty-one-story condominium complex. The builders had to anticipate that someday a hurricane *might* bear down on this stretch of beach, perhaps even on this very building. The building's survival will depend on a deep foundation and a network of reinforcements of concrete and steel throughout the structure.

Why do some dreams crack under pressure, while others, under the same pressure, come out battered but stronger?

In 1982 water-skimming Exocet missiles launched by Argen-

tine planes bypassed radar defenses and sank two British war-
ships in the Falklands war. Military experts were stunned.
Suddenly, blimps or dirigibles were back in. Why? Because they
can sail below radar, almost undetected, whereas enemies can
detect missiles up to 120 miles away, farther than other intelli-
gence devices.

In the age of advanced missile technology, there is a place for
an idea that has been around since the Civil War. Aren't blimps
"sitting targets"? Yes, but they are very durable. One expert,
Alan G. Birchmore of Airship Industries, claimed that even if
four missiles tore through the new ship's skin, its helium would
leak out so slowly that the captain could put on a pot of coffee
and say to the crew, "'O.K., what are we going to do when we
hit the ocean?'"

If the new blimps pass the navy tests, some suggest ultimate
sales could, in the next fifteen years, reach $3 billion. Others
suggest higher figures, because other nations would follow the
U.S. lead.[3]

But dreamers find additional uses as they wait for the military to act. Some of the blimps have been leased to the Fuji Film
Company. Airship, Ltd., has attracted sightseers for a one-hour
air tour of London, blimp-style. The blimp was booked solid
for two months at $145 a person and 4,000 Londoners had
rainchecks. So the dream that seemed forever extinguished
when the *Hindenberg* exploded in 1937 has been resurrected
by some dreamers.[4]

Take another example. When the Arabs raised the price of oil
in the early 1970s, many people predicted the demise of the
cruise lines. The fuel costs would be prohibitive. Yet now, after
TV's "Love Boat," cruising is more popular than ever. New, bigger, more luxurious ships are being built to handle the increased demand. Just stand in the Miami airport some Friday
or Saturday and watch the thousands of people arriving for
their dream cruise. Or stand on the decks and count the number of "I can't believe we're here's!" The dream has been resurrected.

Behind both developments—the blimp and the cruise
ships—are corporate visionaries: dreamers who have refused to

toss in the towel; dreamers who have dared to dismiss the economic forecasts and predictions of "experts"; dreamers who are paid to find ways to make dreams happen; dreamers who have learned to navigate whatever life, war, the economy, or an oil cartel dishes out.

In this chapter I want to identify some principles that will help refurbish or resurrect the dream.

## PRINCIPLE ONE:  DECIDE TO SURVIVE AND TO THRIVE

I believe in survivability. I look back on my own personal nightmare, an unwanted divorce in 1976, my "trial by fire." If anyone had then predicted my survivability—let alone my thrivability—I would have laughed in disbelief. But somewhere en route to a divorce court in a small mountain town in North Carolina, I decided to survive the experience of divorce. And today, as I write this book, I can testify that I survived my big "It."

Out of that tragedy I formulated a simple philosophy of life: *Nothing can happen to me, today, that I will be unable to survive.* "It" may be unpleasant, unfair, humiliating, uncomfortable, but the only way It will defeat me, is *if I agree* to be defeated. In 1976, 1.2 million persons went through divorces, but not all of them survived the experience. Why? Some made a decision to throw in the towel. Some decided to become victims.

At some point in a trial-by-fire, we realize that there is more at stake than we initially assumed. The real issue is always surviving and turning the bad into good. Someone has said that there are no mistakes in life, only lessons. I agree. When *you* decide to label a painful experience a "lesson," you've taken a gigantic step toward survival and toward healing.

Look at the Nazi death camps. Millions of Jews were brutalized, dehumanized, robbed of their rights, dignity, and possessions. Some died, but not always from gas or bullets or starvation. Many gave up. Quit. Succumbed to the Nazi propaganda that they were the earth's garbage and that no one cared about their fate.

One man did not give up. When the Nazis destroyed his

manuscript and life's work, he vowed to live to rewrite it, to improve it. He worked daily on the project in the safety of his imagination. As a result of that determination, the world got the principles of logotherapy. Victor Frankl made his name famous in psychology through *Man in Search of Meaning,* the book he rewrote. Why? Because Frankl chose to survive.[5]

Three thousand years earlier, Jeremiah wrote to a group of Jewish prisoners who were well known for their music, yet were so depressed they could not sing. When their captors demanded a song, the Jews responded bitterly, "How shall we sing the Lord's song in a strange land?"[6]

Strange lands still exist: bankruptcy, divorce, premature death, theft, embezzlement, loss of a job.

Jeremiah answered, "Seek the peace of the city where I have caused you to be carried away captive, and pray to the LORD for it."[7] If that city prospered, so also did those who lived there, whether citizens or captives.

Clearly, the clue for survival in slavery was given to the Hebrews even *before* their captivity when Moses predicted that the Jews would go into pagan lands, marry pagan wives, and eventually worship pagan gods. The Jews loudly disputed his predictions. *Never!*

Yet Moses offered words of encouragement, heard by the realists in the group. "But from there you will seek the LORD your God, and you will find Him if you seek Him with all your heart and with all your soul."[8]

Two words that offered so much promise to them offer as much promise to us today: *"from there* you will find Him."

Where's your "there" as you read this? The prophecy is the same. Your current "there" is a good place to launch your dream. I'm not an expert at hockey, but I have concluded that a player's being ordered off the ice and into the penalty box is not always a penalty. For some, the penalty box has been a place to catch their breath. Some players have returned to the ice and helped win a game after their rest, or penalty "off the ice."

I realize it may not be easy for you to accept this. You may even be constructing a "yes . . . but" answer as you read. Nevertheless, if you would spend as much time embracing this principle as picking out its flaws, you might see how well it works.

Consider the story of an accountant who was told that he was going blind. How would he support his family? One day, depressed and in despair, he sat munching on a doughnut when he suddenly snarled, "I think even I could make a better doughnut than this!"

Harry Winker did just that. He founded the Mr. Donut chain. Doughnuts kept his family fed. Harry Winker survived blindness and his "Oh, no!" because he decided to survive and to thrive.

I think of a shoe stitcher in Dixon, Illinois, who lost three of his fingers to a shoe machine. How would he support his family? He no longer had the dexterity to turn the shoes, to stitch as many shoes per shift. He made a decision to survive. He became an assistant to the pharmacist who had stitched his stubs. An "Oh, no!" didn't defeat Charles Walgreen. He eventually founded his own chain of drug stores and became wealthy.[9]

What is your "Oh, no!" You can control this situation because you have the power to survive.

## PRINCIPLE TWO: GIVE YOURSELF TIME TO HEAL

In November 1963 this nation marveled at the calm composure of Jackie Kennedy during the funeral of her young husband, President John F. Kennedy, a dreamer who had talked about Camelot. This dreamer had dared to challenge a generation of dreamers with his inaugural words, "Ask not what your country can do for you, but ask what *you can do for your country*" (italics mine).

Mrs. Kennedy's conduct sparked a lot of discussion during and after the funeral. However, her choice was similar to that of many widows who simply "take charge" of the experience. They do not throw themselves on their husband's funeral pyre and die, too, as in some cultures.

Ultimately, widows have to have a period of recovery, of healing. In my seminars with divorced people I say that they will need two to four years for recovery. "What!" many howl in protest. But I've known enough people to know that those who try to skip the time-out end up as statistics on second- and third-time divorce charts.

Some people turn to counselors as part of the healing process. I strongly applaud their courage. However, a few expect counselors to be "Mr. Fix Its" who will, in one or two sessions, "do the trick."

Healing refuses to be rushed. I remember after surgery, I was amazed by how quickly the surface incision healed. However, below the surface, an inferno of infection boiled. I was sicker than I thought because I observed only the surface.

Why are we so impatient? The Jews have a process called *ninyan,* whereby friends physically feed the widow or widower after a funeral. The bereaved can accept such hospitality because they know that someday the roles will be reversed. The one who is fed today will someday spoon down the hot soup for another. I think we need a similar response for broken dreams. Mourning is a legitimate part of the healing process.

One of the great stories of courage in the Old Testament is Jacob's fleeing his brother's threat to kill him. On the run, hoping to find refuge with his uncle, he made camp one night in a lonesome place. He dreamed of a stairway reaching into the heavens. The Lord said to this thief, Jacob, who had deceived his father into granting him the blessing rightfully his brother's:

> I am the LORD God of Abraham your father and the God of Isaac; the land on which you lie I will give to you and to your descendants. Also your descendants shall be as the dust of the earth; you shall spread abroad to the west and the east, to the north and the south; and in you and in your seed all the families of the earth shall be blessed. Behold, I am with you and will keep you wherever you go, and will bring you back to this land; for I will not leave you until I have done what I have spoken to you.[10]

Jacob could only respond, "Surely the LORD is in this place, and I did not know it."[11]

That statement could be spoken by a thousand people today,

exhausted in their grief, disappointment, or humiliation. The Lord wants to be in your tragedies and traumas as well as in your triumphs. The difference between a tragedy and a triumph is often decided by our recognition of God's willingness to resurrect the dream in the most unlikely places and through the most unlikely resources.

I call such moments crossroads or intersections. They offer us the opportunity to decide I'm either going to get bitter or better! to be a victor or a victim!

The healing process can either rekindle one's hope or nourish one's resentment. The healing process gives you time to decide which way you will channel your energies: toward yesterday or toward tomorrow. It's your choice.

**PRINCIPLE THREE: GET COUNSELING**

A dreamburst may provide clues about what went wrong, enough clues to help insure that the experience is not repeated. In many books that I autograph, I like to write this phrase: *Ashes nourish dreams*. I believe that it is possible to find in the wreckage the knowledge that will help us build tomorrow. That's why scientists painstakingly go over experiment failures to determine why something failed. That's why the FAA conducts thorough on-site inspections of every air crash. That's why doctors do autopsies.

Sometimes we are too close to the crisis. We are biased. That's why the airlines cannot investigate their crashes alone. They would be looking for evidence to prove that they were not guilty of negligence or human error. The FAA team is there to be impartial.

Often in our anguish, we need another's insight and guidance, one who can say, "Oh, it isn't that bad!" or who can cut short our diatribes with a well-timed, "Yes, but . . ." In the devastation of the fire that destroyed his laboratory, Thomas Edison needed a Henry Ford. What would have happened to the inventor if Ford had not come forward?

I have been impressed by the number of retired business executives who work as volunteer counselors through the Small

Business Administration. They freely share their time and skills to help struggling entrepreneurs make it.

Don't try to be a lone ranger. Seek counseling.

## PRINCIPLE FOUR: LOOK FOR OTHERS IN THE SAME SITUATION

I have spent a lot of time working with single adults, many of whom are divorced. The process of divorce recovery is helpful because we can help each other heal. We need to cash in our self-sufficiency. People who have been there have the most credibility as guides and encouragers.

One of my companies, Tear-Catchers, a Ministry of Compassion, is designed to encourage "sympathetic suffering and sharing." I encourage people to take their pain and use it to touch others. Your yesterday is someone's today. This phrase is on my stationery: *Your tears can be an oasis for the next weary pilgrim.* I believe that.

Listen to this description of loss:

My new office was little more than a cubicle with a small desk and a telephone. My secretary was already there, with tears in her eyes. Without saying a word, she pointed to the cracked linoleum floor and the two plastic coffee cups on the desk. Only yesterday, she and I had been working in the lap of luxury. The office of the president was the size of a grand hotel suite. I had my own bathroom. I even had my own living quarters. . . . I was served by white-coated waiters who were on call all day. I once brought some relatives from Italy to see where I worked, and they thought they had died and gone to heaven. . . .

For me *this* was Siberia. It was exile to the farthest corner of the kingdom.

This final humiliation was much worse than being fired. It was enough to make me want to kill—I wasn't quite sure who.[12]

How many businessmen and would-be entrepreneurs have taken courage from Lee Iacocca, who wrote those words *after* he was fired as president of Ford Motor Company?

His dream exploded and shattered into a million pieces, or so he thought *at the time*. Instead, it was only one chapter. The best was yet to come: the presidency of Chrysler, a bestseller, TV commercials, and talk of a run for the presidency of the United States. His firing was only a detour.

Perhaps you want to know why you should have to take a detour, a time-out, en route to your dream?

Reality is not always a convenient interrupter of our dreams and dream schedules. Besides, this detour may set the stage for you to mentor another's dream. Iacocca has a permanent niche in American folklore, more so than many of the professional after-dinner "motivational" lecturers. Why? He's been there. Dream strugglers can identify with him.

I think of one motivational speaker. Thousands hear him annually and buy his tapes and books. Yet many go away unimpressed. Why? He has it made. It's been too long on the gravy train for him. He's forgotten the detour in his life. He's forgotten his "then."

We're all familiar with the three *R*'s of education: reading, 'riting, and 'rithmetic. I would suggest that there are three *R*'s for restoring the dream: repair, resurrect, and redefine.

### Repair

I well remember the childhood days I spent struggling to repair deflated bicycle tires and basketballs. It's amazing what either can do to a boy's morale. I've also broken things that have more sentimental than economic value, things that could not be easily repaired or replaced. In such moments it is easy to snarl, "Things can't be like they were!" Iacocca could have said that. Instead, I insist that things (however you define *things*) *can be better*. So why would you settle for their being *the same*?

Sometimes the best repair cannot be easily accomplished. It takes time and requires more than the equivalent of Elmer's glue. So may it be with the patchwork on your dream.

### Resurrect

Dead dreams can come back to life.

One of the most heatedly debated events in the world is the bodily resurrection of Jesus. Some have attempted to diminish the incredible by suggesting that he was merely in a coma or a trance. The apostle Paul declared, "*that same power* that raised Jesus Christ from the dead" is available to you and to me.[13] The power that created the Pacific Ocean and the Smoky Mountains, the surf and the sunsets, is available to you and to me. Today. That's incredible! *That same power* exists, according to my friend Tony Campolo, "to equip us to be God's agents for change in this present age," to transform us into fearless dreamers and "doers of those things we believe God wants us to do."[14]

At times, executives have been brought in to shape up a division or plant or company and then were denied the resources to make the change happen. But we have the power to realize our dreams. So why don't more of our dreams become a reality?

Charles Converse offered an explanation in the hymn "What a Friend We Have in Jesus", with the line, "Oh what peace we often forfeit, / Oh what needless pain we bear." Why? "All because we do not carry, / Everything [including our dream and schedule] to God in prayer."[15] It only takes a slight amendment to the hymn to say, "Oh what power [the same power that resurrected Jesus from the dead] we often forfeit, *because we try to do it ourselves.*"

Someone shared the story with me about a bricklayer who had an accident on a construction site and had to supply additional information to the insurance company as to why the accident occurred:

> I'm a bricklayer by trade. On the date of the accident I was working alone on the roof of a new six-story building. When I completed my work I discovered that I had about five hundred pounds of brick left over. Rather than carry the bricks down by hand, I decided to lower them in a barrel (using a pulley that was fortunately attached to the side of the building at the sixth floor). Once I had secured the rope at ground level, I went up to the roof, swung the barrel out, and loaded the bricks into it. Then I went back to the ground and untied the rope, holding the rope tightly to insure a slow descent of the five hundred pounds of bricks.
>
> You will note in block #2 of the accident report form that I

stated that I weigh 135 pounds. Due to my surprise at being jerked off the ground so suddenly, I lost my presence of mind and forgot to let go of the rope. Needless to say, I proceeded at a rather rapid rate up the side of the building. In the vicinity of the third floor, I met the barrel coming down. This explains the fractured skull and broken collar bone.

Slowed down only slightly, I continued my rapid ascent, not stopping until my right hand was two knuckles deep into the pulley. Fortunately, I had regained my presence of mind and was able to hold tightly to the rope in spite of my pain.

At approximately the same time, however, the barrel of bricks hit the ground and the bottom fell out of the barrel. Devoid of the weight of the bricks, the barrel now weighed approximately 50 pounds. I refer you again to my weight in block #2. As you might imagine, I began a rather rapid descent down the side of the building. In the vicinity of the 3rd floor, I again met the barrel coming up. This accounts for my two fractured ankles and the lacerations of my leg and lower body. This encounter with the barrel slowed me enough to lessen my injuries when I fell onto the pile of bricks. Fortunately, only three of my vertebrae were cracked.

I'm sorry to report, however, as I lay there on the bricks, unable to stand, watching the empty barrel six stories above me, I again lost my presence of mind and let go of the rope. The empty barrel weighed more than the rope so it came back down and broke both of my legs.

I hope that I have furnished the information that you require as to how the accident occurred because I *was trying to do the job alone*.

What is true of bricks is also true of dreams. And what is true of bricklayers is true of dreamers. You will need the help of others to resurrect your dream.

### Redefine

Sometimes brokenness and rejection lead us to further examine our dreams, or to redefine our dreams. After my loss, I may be better able to clarify my goal and to bring it into sharper and clearer focus.

The junk heap of dreams is stacked too high with discarded, crumpled dreams. I don't want you to join that status. Your courage during this dreamstorm or setback or disappointment may give you time to catch your breath, to wipe the sweat or tears from your eyes, to tighten your grasp on your dream, and again to resume the fight to bring your dream to birth.

~~~~~~~~~~~~~~~~~~~~~~~~~~~~

1. Do you agree with the author's statement, "Nothing can happen to me, today, that I will be unable to survive"?

2. What painful experiences have you labeled "lessons"?

3. Why is mourning a loss part of the healing process?

4. What loss(es) are you mourning?

5. Have you gotten counseling for your loss? If not, what has kept you from seeking counseling?

6. Can things always "be better"?

7. What is one situation or relationship you now experience as "better"?

8. If you had the opportunity, what is one of your dreams you would like to restore? What prevents that from happening?

# 9

# BE CAREFUL TO BALANCE THE DREAM

I enjoy vacationing in Key West, Florida, the "last resort" or the "Conch Republic." There is a sense in which you leave time in the Miami airport. While there, I love to lie in the sun and relax. Then, about sundown, I like to wander down Duval Street, browsing in the T-shirt shops, making my way toward Mallory Square, where hundreds of locals and tourists gather to watch the sunset. Some nights the sunset is beyond description.

A number of artists gather to entertain the tourists. One of my favorites is a juggler. He forms a circle with a rope, then invites everyone to step in and watch his show.

I quickly learned that I didn't have the gift of juggling. In fact, I suspect most people don't; otherwise, the guy at Mallory Square could never make a living. No one would say, "Wouldja look at that!"

In a sense, handling dreams is like juggling the past, the present, and the future. You must find the right mix of these three volatile elements, which will either make you or break you and your dream.

Haven't you met compulsive dreamers? All they can talk about is "someday, when *my* dream comes true." They have no sense of yesterday and little sense of today. Everything is tomorrow. Furthermore, they don't listen to what you say unless it is directly related to their dream. And even then . . .

Webster defines *balance* as "to bring into harmony or proportion." You may think of an old scale on which the standard measure was put on one side and the item to be weighed on the other. How many scales were significantly out of balance?

That happens with dreamers, particularly those who believe they are pursuing the dream *for* somebody. Once the dream is reality, they believe they will be able to compensate for all the lost time. But some families cannot wait that long; children grow up. That's one reason Harry Chapin's song "Cat in the Cradle" was so popular. It zinged its way into the consciousness of many fast-trackers.

Too often it is the *second* wife and the *second* family who enjoy the fruits of a dreamer's productivity. And some dreamers never quite get over the guilt residue. They may be able to financially make it up to individuals, but it's never quite the same.

Five elements are important in balancing the dream.

## 1. COUNTING THE COST(S)

Once you're several years into a dream, you need to ask yourself, *How much is this dream costing me?* I have author friends who decided to do a five-day-a-week, fifteen-minute radio program. Everyone said it would be a "go."

Later, after they were all but forced to file for bankruptcy, they admitted they had underestimated the costs of the dream. Once they got into it, the costs kept escalating like a monster that couldn't be fed enough. When they discovered that I, too, was considering radio, they responded, "Listen to the consultants; then *double* their estimates."

Dreams have an incredible suction on time. For example, the dreamer and you may be in a great restaurant. Halfway through the meal, you sense that only about 25 percent of the dreamer is sitting across from you. The body may be there, but the mind and heart are elsewhere.

The story is told that when Thomas Edison remarried, he was so used to going to his lab at all hours of the night and day, he asked his bride on their wedding night if she would mind if he went over to the lab "for a little while." "No," she answered.

Hours later, one of Edison's assistants drove by the lab and saw lights. Immediately, he suspected burglars. Imagine his surprise when he discovered Edison at work.

"Mr. Edison, this is your wedding night! What are you doing here?"

The inventor looked puzzled. "Oh yes," he said, and calmly left the lab.

I suspect there were many other such nights for Mrs. Edison. On the other hand, Edison still holds the record for the most patents (1,093) granted to one person.[1]

How many have discovered that the pursuit of their dream is like a sponge, always soaking up more?

I look at some of the bright young lawyers currently implicated in the Wall Street insider trading scandals. Martin Siegel, former takeover chief at Kidder, Peabody, had it all: Connecticut estate, million-dollar Manhattan condo, family, a reputation, and most importantly, a future. Apparently that wasn't enough. Siegel accepted large sums of cash, perhaps $700,000, from Ivan Boesky, in exchange for inside information about corporate takeovers between June 1984 and January 1986. Now he is barred from working in the securities business, and he has agreed to "disgorge" at least $9 million for restitution to the investors who were cheated by his actions.[2]

Since then, there has been a chain reaction: one exdreamer financier pointing the finger at another. And the public's confidence has been shaken in Wall Street.

Isn't it possible that this man, as he stood on street corners, waiting for a courier carrying a briefcase stuffed with cash, thought about his future? Did he count the cost? If he had been a poor man, perhaps it might be easier to understand. But in 1985, Siegel legitimately earned $1.7 million. Shouldn't that have been *enough?*[3]

We are experiencing an explosion of greed in our society. Greed is an obsession with counting one's wealth while ignoring the costs of acquiring the wealth.

Greed has always been a part of the system. We have enshrined our American heritage and the founding fathers, but several Indian tribes did not hold our ancestors in as high esteem. Still there was some sense of decency. For example, when the robber barons and tycoons made too much money in the late 1880s and 1890s, an era of reform was ushered in by presidents Theodore Roosevelt and William Howard Taft.

Today's mutant of greed is unmitigated. Financial editors charged in an article in *M: The Civilized Man* that Americans work in "a complete absence of any sense of propriety, ethics or guilt to keep the desire in check. Hardly anyone learns about the Seven Deadly Sins anymore." Many see greed as "just part of the game."[4]

What is also different is the presence of two realities: upward mobility and downward mobility, or downsizing. All across corporate America the emphasis is on cutting costs and downsizing. Suddenly, job security in middle management is tenuous. There is no longer a guarantee that you will get the gold watch. IBM, for example, has reduced its work force 7 percent; AT&T recently cut 32,000 from its staff to save $1 billion. That cut meant the loss of 11,600 management positions. CBS pruned away 1,200 of its 15,500 workers.[5]

"Here today gone tomorrow" has new implications, which has led some to adopt an economic strategy to get it while the getting's good. For those with a bent toward greed, it means grab all you can and never mind what people think.

I recently spoke in San Jose, which has more than its fair share of yuppies and entrepreneurs. The question there isn't "Why aren't you rich?" but "Why haven't you started your own company?"

Americans believe that money covers a lot of excesses. If you don't believe that, walk into a bookstore and look at all the books on how to make money.

But Jesus asked a simple question: "What will a man give in exchange for his soul?"[6] That still bears consideration. You can have it all and have a barren desert in the corridors of your heart.

Counting the cost implies decision making at every stage. Americans were so quick to believe that the *next* escalation of troops in Vietnam was going to win the war. Always the next. So it is with the *next* salary raise, the *next* promotion, the *next* transfer.

Ask yourself the following questions, developed by philosopher Alfred Montapert:

- Am I doing the things that make me happy?
- Are my thoughts of noble character?
- How can I simplify my life?
- What are my talents?
- Does my work [dream] satisfy my soul?
- Am I giving value to my existence?
- How can I improve my life?[7]

Too often dreamers count the costs in mere dollars and cents. There are other criteria, equally important, in the balancing of your dream.

## 2. ANTICIPATING THE CONSEQUENCES

People in Kansas City are still talking about "The Wedding," which took place at Unity on the Plaza. After the ceremony, the couple, in a cherry-red Rolls, led a motorcade downtown as they were serenaded by a marching band. When the couple arrived at the reception, two thousand guests crammed into a hotel ballroom equipped with a full-sized carousel, a gift for the bride.

In front of an American flag, Del Dunmire, the groom, led the guests in singing "The Star Spangled Banner" and "God Bless America." Then he gave $350,000 to charities, trusts, and scholarship programs. Next, Del pledged $1 million to fight drugs. Afterward, Frankie Avalon, Bobby Rydell, and Fabian sang the hits of the fifties.

The groom rented five hundred rooms in the Vista Hotel so guests could stay if they were tired after the reception.

Yes, Del Dunmire has the money to pay for all of it. His company, Growth Industries in Grandview, Missouri, makes replacement parts for commercial airliners and is doing quite well.[8]

No, he wasn't neglecting his business or his employees or other charities.

Yes, he wanted to give his bride something she would long remember (if she forgets, she has eighty-eight hours of video tapes to refresh her memory).

But his dream has had incredible consequences. In less than twelve months he has become Kansas City's number one philanthropist, and politicians from Topeka to Washington, D.C., return his phone calls. Senators now invite him to their swearing-in ceremonies, whereas twelve months ago they didn't know his name or that he existed. Today, he could underwrite their next dream.

There's nothing wrong with that; IOU's are a basic part of American political and economic life.

However, Debbie Dunmire has learned that wealthy looks different from how it feels. "I think that wealthy people have all the problems other people have, plus one: money and the fear of losing it." She awakens some mornings, after a dream that "someone" has taken it all away from them.

Her phone rings constantly with invitations. She never has to have an empty calendar. In fact, they have hired a retired Secret Service agent, who works harder now than he ever did at the White House.

Debbie Dunmire, in an interview with the *Kansas City Star,* said she understands how comedian Freddie Printz must have felt on his "rocket ride to stardom." She confided, "Everybody wants to be famous but I didn't know how wearing it is."[9] The young bride is discovering that even a star-spangled, well-financed dream can be a bumpy ride.

Oddly, there is a common expression that summarizes this response: *I never dreamed it would end up this way.* So some take the exit that Freddie Printz chose.

Success has consequences. How are you "wearing" your dream?

### 3. MEASURING THE STRESS

Look at Leontyne Price, the black daughter of a sawmill worker and a midwife. She won a scholarship to Julliard; then she was discovered by the great American composer, Virgil Thompson. No one handed her an operatic career on a silver platter. She said, "I am here [where I am] and you will know that I am the best. The color of my skin or the kink of my hair has nothing to do with what you are listening to." She had to endure racial slurs and innuendos.[10]

She decided somewhere on her rise to stardom that she could survive the stress, whereas others would have given up and bought a Greyhound bus ticket home to Laurel, Mississippi, mumbling, "It's not worth it!"

If Leontyne had not survived the stress and paid the price, it would have been more difficult for other black women to achieve their dreams.

I have often driven over the San Francisco-Oakland Bay Bridge, which is eight and a quarter miles long and links rural areas to San Francisco, creating its bedroom neighborhoods. Built during the depression, the bridge took three years to construct and claimed twenty-nine lives. Men went to work realizing that they could be the next casualty. John Kergel, who worked on the span, said, "Guys would do anything for a job. We took a lot of chances. But it paid off." To John the real consequence is this: "What's important is that during the Great Depression people had the vision and the gumption to build" such a bridge. But first it was a dream in a lot of people's minds.[11]

You have to befriend the stress. Harry Truman often quipped, "If you can't stand the heat, get out of the kitchen."

I think of Gordon Gould, an inventor who has lived with stress in a twenty-seven year battle to win the patent right to the laser. He has spent $2.5 million ($100,000 out of his own pocket) for attorney's fees. As a graduate student at Columbia University, in 1957 he discovered the laser, or what he called "the fire." Because he misunderstood the process, however, he did not apply for a patent until 1959. By that time, two other scientists had already filed applications and were awarded the patents.

Gould dropped out of Columbia and fought the Patent Office over the products of his research. Meanwhile, those with the patents were making millions of dollars that Gould argued were rightfully his.

In 1986 a federal court ordered the U.S. Patent Office to reverse itself and award Gould a patent for the gas-discharge laser used in operating rooms, supermarket checkout lanes, and in compact disc players. That patent could produce $20 to $30 million in royalties per year. In a bureaucracy and a scientific community, this scientist "measured the stress" and hung in the fight.[12]

## 4. APPLAUDING ANOTHER'S DREAM

Getting ahead and keeping up with the Joneses are common goals in our competitive society. Each rung of the success ladder seems more narrow as the climber moves up with one eye focused above and one behind to be aware of any competitor who is gaining ground.

Workers sabotage colleagues' work. Professional jealousy and grandstanding are commonplace. Dog-eat-dog and rat-race thinking prevail. I saw a sign which observed, "Even if you win the rat race—you're still a rat."

Reality says that some superachievers are smug, conceited, arrogant prima donnas, mumbling, "How sweet it is."

Sometimes I am called upon to celebrate another's best seller. Other times I have lost out for writing prizes and awards, although I believed that my work was superior. How could I applaud for another? Maybe that's why I love to watch the Oscar and Emmy ceremonies. The cameras pan the audiences as the list of nominees is read; the excitement builds. "The envelope, please." The presenter rips it open and smiles. "The winner is . . ." One shot puts all the nominees on the screen at one time. Smiles, surprise, tears on the winner's face. However, the camera also captures the losers' faces. We in the audience delight in deciphering their expressions. What did he or she really feel?

That's the same reason I hate the concession speeches on election night, especially when the race has been close.

A dreamer must be willing to applaud another's dream, to discipline his or her own reactions. Yes, it's easy to cast an aspersion on another's achievement. Certainly it hurts to lose. But I must not forget that my dream will be delayed, perhaps permanently, if I try to simultaneously nourish resentment and a dreamseed. Resentment will always dominate.

Perhaps you saw the movie *Amadeus,* the story of the musical genius, Mozart. Were you infuriated by his conniving and scheming competitor, Salieri?

Although Mozart seemingly captured the music of the heavens, Salieri always dismissed his compositions as amateurish. Even Mozart's best drew a "yes, but" qualifier from Salieri.

Yet, today, no one would pay to see a movie or play entitled *Salieri.* Why? Salieri's music was second rate, poisoned by the composer's hatred of Mozart's incredible talent.

Will someone in the distant future find a similarity between you and Salieri? Start the applause. Praise is like a boomerang. You start it, and it will return to you.

Can you enthusiastically applaud another's dream? Every moment spent sulking over another's success is a moment that could have been invested in yours. Thus your success is delayed a second, a moment, or forever by your petulance.

Keep competition, when necessary, within reason. Monitor yourself and ask others to watch you. Remember, your attitude will be showing. Run the geiger counter across your project for the tell-tale signs of envy.

The world is always ready for another best seller, movie-of-the-year, or breakthrough. *Yours.*

Foster a competitive spirit. Be the first to applaud your competition.

## 5. DEFINING SUCCESS

What is a successful dream? How do you define it? How will you know when you have found it?

- Ten million dollars in the bank?
- Never to have to work again?
- Fame?
- Recognition?
- Power?

The likelihood of your reaching your dream, whatever it is, is proportional to your awareness and approach to this principle: A dream is a pilgrimage, not a destination.

Landing crafts are designed to transport troops from the ship to the beach. The beach, however, is not the ultimate destination. The jungle, two hundred yards to the north, needs to be taken. Tragically, some troops have been marched up and down the beach rather than up into enemy territory. Some of us have landed on the beaches of a thousand dreams but have never moved on to possess the promised land.

Remember how proud Americans were of the Mercury space program?

Remember how proud Americans were of the Project Apollo launches?

Remember how proud Americans were of the first *Challenger* space shuttle?

Someday permanent space stations and colonization will be commonplace. We will look back on our earlier achievements as simplistic. Who knows what possibilities and dreams swirl in the imaginations and fantasies of NASA scientists? Dreams that, even if a scientist shared them with me, would leave me befuddled, perhaps labeling them as science fiction.

So many have reached their dreams but have wasted their pilgrimages, too bored or too fatigued to enjoy the success once they arrive. How many build their dream house and die before they can enjoy it? How many work to build a nest egg yet die before or soon after retirement? How many have their dreams but find the aftertaste sour or bitter?

Harold S. Kushner said it well in his best seller, *When All You've Ever Wanted Isn't Enough*. Clearly, the attainment of your dream, if perceived solely as a destination, will never satisfy your deepest longings.[13] It's how you live your life en route to your dream that counts. The dog-eat-doggers, the rat packers, the elbowers-under-the-basketers only punish themselves.

I contend that the quest for the dream can be fun.

### What Is Real Success to You?

Dreamers need frequently to ask themselves that question. Scully Blotnick said that Americans measure success in four ways: *fame, fortune, prestige,* and *power.* Forget the Boy Scout definition of happiness, marriage, and family.[14]

Leo Braudy explored the success factors in *The Frenzy of Re-*

*nown: Fame and Its History.* He concluded that "fame is really our religion in America, and we have a constantly changing calendar of saints." In fact, some dreamers cannot enjoy their success as they scramble up the ladder of success because they hear the intense breathing of the person on the rung below them.[15]

He added, "Increasingly ordinary people seem to feel that without fame they are somehow incomplete. . . . People see someone on the TV screen and think: Why can't I be up there, too? If people do not pay attention to you, you feel as if you don't exist."

As more "ordinary" people reach their dreams, they have to grapple with the companions to dreams. Blotnick says that there is a common myth that people who immediately achieve in their businesses really lack management skills. Once the company grows to be too big for them, they no longer know how to run it.

Not so, says Blotnick. "They go belly-up because they dip into the company bank account too soon and too deeply so they can support themselves and their [families] in the grand manner to which they've become accustomed."[16] Some are "trying to make it up" for those long, lean years—for missed baseball games and piano recitals.

Secondly, they learn that success can quickly become past tense. What matters is what you have done lately. That's why Americans love entrepreneurs, the rags-to-riches movers and shakers more than the equally rich who had wealthy fathers and mothers and inherited their loot.

They also learn that there is always someone with more or better. That's one reality that made the "Beverly Hillbillies" such a popular TV show in the 60s. How could these hillbillies from West Virginia survive in Hollywood?

Whose standard will you use: the Colbys'? J. R. Ewing's? Blake Carrington's? Someone's you have seen on "Lifestyles of the Rich and Famous"? Or that distinctive inner voice you recognize?

Blotnick insists that the world demands that success be measured quantitatively—in performance or in dollars and cents.[17]

I was struck by reading biographical materials on Tom Monaghan. Yes, it was incredible when his Tigers won the World Series. It's one thing to own a baseball team, an expensive "hobby"; it's another to own winners.

Success for him was not measured just by gate receipts. For example, Monaghan made a difficult decision to close a section of bleachers where rowdy fans had been chanting obscenities in unison. He could have had a Tiger stadium attendance record, but his definition of success made room for decency.

When asked what he makes of his "dream life" in the material world, he said, "Improving my spiritual life is still my first priority. We Catholics believe that the only way to get to Heaven is to die in a state of sanctified grace, without any unforgiven mortal sins against us. And I believe that too. Because if Hell exists, I don't want to go there."[18]

Sometimes there are "surprise" definitions of success. The laser researcher, Gordon Gould, discovered that at age sixty-five. One would think that after so long a struggle and after the kind of money the court awarded him, he would be living extravagantly. No. He said, "How can you spend that kind of money on your private life?" He plans instead to use the money to finance exploration of the many inventions that still buzz inside his brain.

The real measure of his success was personal. When Gould developed a detached retina in his right eye, two immediate operations *with a laser* saved his eyesight.[19]

Ralph Waldo Emerson said it best when he observed:

A person is a success
who has lived well, laughed often, and loved much;
who has gained the respect of intelligent men and the love
of children;
who has filled his niche and accomplished his task;
who leaves the world better than he found it, whether by
an improved poppy, a perfect poem, or a rescued soul;
who never lacked appreciation of earth's beauty or failed
to express it;

who looked for the best in others and gave the best all he had.[20]

Harold Kushner suggested that our greed is fueled by a fear of death. Grabbing "all the gusto" we can, while we can, in the words of one commercial.

Kushner said:

> I have no fear of death because I feel that I have lived. I have loved and I have been loved. I have been challenged in my personal and professional life and have managed, if not a perfect score, at least a passing grade and perhaps a little bit better than that.[21]

He asked a question that all dreamers should daily attempt to answer: "What are the things you *absolutely* must have and do so that you can feel that you have lived your life and have not wasted it?"

Now what are you going to do with your answer? It is possible to gain the whole world, or at least a significant chunk of it. But the experience so far has been that it is only yours for the moment. Someday, it will belong to someone else.

In a book entitled *Restoring Your Spiritual Passion,* Gordon MacDonald addressed the menace of workaholism—always in the realm of possibility for the dreamer. He decried the common "tendency to use time flagrantly in the building of one's fortune at the expense of a more balanced and spiritually oriented life."[22]

Here today; gone tomorrow. Today's billionaire tycoons and deal makers will join a long list: John D. Rockefeller, John Jacob Astor, J. P. Morgan, Cornelius Vanderbilt, Jay Gould, Andrew Carnegie, J. Paul Getty, Andrew Mellon—none of whom bought immortality.

I was struck by the closing paragraph in an article on Del Dunmire. "You've got to provide the element of hope. That's what hell is: life without hope." Del admitted that he's still afraid of his "end." He confessed, "When I'm out there on the street with my tin cup, I just wonder how many of my friends that our company and our charities have done something for will throw a quarter in my cup. Maybe nobody."[23]

Now may be the time to formulate your doctrine of success. For when your dream comes in, your phone, like Del Dunmire's, may be ringing too.

~~~~~~~~~~~~~~~~~~~~~

1. How much is your dream costing you?

2. How prevalent is greed in our world? Is it exaggerated or underestimated?

3. How prevalent is greed in your life?

4. Are you doing the things that make you happy?

5. Does your dream satisfy you?

6. Are there areas in your life where "when/then" thinking is influential?

7. What are the ways you could simplify your life?

8. Why is it so difficult to applaud another's dream?

9. Think of one of your friends or associates. How could you applaud his or her dream?

10. How do you define success? Answer these statements:

   I am a success if
   I am a success when

I am a success because
I am a success unless

11. Will the attainment of your dream satisfy you?

12. What are the things you absolutely must have and do to feel that you have lived your life and have not wasted it?

# 10

# NURTURE THE NEXT GENERATION OF DREAMERS

The story is told of a man wandering through a desert, dying of thirst. He came upon a small cistern, a cup of water, and a note. The note read, "You have a choice. You can drink this water and eventually will probably die of thirst. Or you can use this water to prime the pump and have all the water you want. If you choose the latter, please refill the cup for the next traveler to choose."

That story introduces us to the ninth step for the dreamer: You must nurture the next generation of dreamers, the children of today.

It doesn't take much listening to the news or reading of newspapers and magazines to understand that it's a tough time to be a child or a teenager. Major problems exist in our nation's educational system at all levels. In an era of unprecedented opportunities, not all children have equal access to the chance to develop to their potentials and to pursue their dreams. That reality should bother dreamers. What can a dreamer do to nurture the next generation of dreamers?

## 1. BE ACQUAINTED WITH THE NEXT GENERATION

In the next decade almost fifty million children will pass through America's eighty thousand elementary schools, the launch pad for their apprenticeship with dreams. Secretary of Education Edward J. Bennett observed, "Overall, elementary education is in pretty good shape; in some measures, our elementary schools are doing a better job now than they have in years. Yet they could and should be better still."[1] They will have to be better to meet the growing tide of foreign competition, particularly from the Japanese whose educational system rigorously prepares the next generation of Japanese dreamers, inventors, and entrepreneurs.

A significant portion of our children are not physically fit. Sixty percent cannot pass minimum fitness requirements of the President's Council on Physical Fitness. A troublesome percentage are being exposed at early ages—as early as third grade—to drugs, a dream's worst enemy.

Particularly threatening, however, is the menace of teenage sexual behavior and pregnancy.

- By age 20, 81 percent of today's unmarried males and 60 percent of unmarried females will have had sex;
- 50 percent of sexually active males had *first* intercourse between the ages of eleven and thirteen;
- in a study published in *Teenage* magazine 99 percent ranked premarital sexual relations as the number one problem facing teens;
- more than 30,000 girls under the age of fifteen will become pregnant this year;
- over one-fourth of all abortions performed in the United States each year are performed on teens. In 1981 teens aged fifteen to nineteen had 433,330 abortions, or more than 1,187 per day;
- most of the babies born to teen mothers will end up on welfare rolls;
- only half of all girls who have their first baby in their teens will finish high school.[2]

That translates into mutilated dreams, dreams that will never be given a fair chance.

How does a dreamer see such depressing statistics? As a problem or as an opportunity? Some doomsayers are predicting dire consequences; others say the statistics have to be understood in light of today, not yesterday. Whatever your interpretation, the problems are there and you need to be involved. Remember, this generation of dreamers will be financing your social security. They will be the captains of industry and finance and diplomacy.

## 2. BE INTERESTED IN THE NEXT GENERATION OF DREAMERS

Why should you be interested? Benjamin Franklin said an ounce of prevention is worth a pound of cure. More concern for and interest in the next generation, especially those in the early grades, will result in fewer dropouts, fewer retentions, and a better prepared and more creative work force and citizenry.

Are you a member of a PTA or a school group? "Oh," you respond, "I don't have any children" or "My children are grown." You still need to be interested in the schooling of today's children. Education Secretary Bennett maintains that an understanding of education has to be extended "beyond the schoolhouse door." Are you interested in the developments in education at the federal, state, and local levels? You should be as a taxpayer and also as a dreamer. Certain areas of education have far-reaching consequences. I'd like to suggest two particular interest areas.

### Interest Area 1: *Philosophies*

At the heart of the debate over education are philosophical differences. Recent comparison between Japanese educational theories and American attitudes is clear. The Japanese believe that *all* children have the same potential for learning; therefore, all children are locked into a sequence of education that becomes increasingly more difficult. Children who fall behind are termed *ochikobore,* meaning "those who have fallen to the bottom." However, the Japanese realistically supplement their system with *juku,* or remedial classes after the regular school day.[3]

The American philosophy, based on our democratic roots, says *all* children can learn *to the extent of their abilities*. However, issues such as race, ethnicity, family structure, and poverty define "extent." There is no *juku* in our system.

Secondly, the Japanese system praises three virtues:

(1) endurance; (2) hard work; and (3) high ambitions. The Japanese students go to school 220 days a year (compared to the Americans' 180); students attend Monday through Friday, with a half day on Saturday. Most students stay an additional hour or two for related club activities.

How many teachers, particularly in low-paying school systems, say, "I'm paid peanuts. Why should I stay after school?" Ask Jeri Antozzi, who teaches at Oldsmar Elementary School near Tampa. In addition to her teaching load in science and math, she is faculty adviser for the school's Young Astronaut Club, which meets Thursdays after school for twelve weeks each school year. Some seventy-five third, fourth, and fifth graders participate in activities such as going on field trips; listening to speakers from industries like Honeywell, which builds components for the space shuttles; and launching their own miniature rockets.

Isn't the third grade a little early to be encouraging children to think of space exploration? No, said Antozzi. "We believe our challenge for the future is the exploration of space. There can be no greater challenge than this."[4]

The club recently sponsored an all-school assembly and invited as speaker Donald L. Chaffee, who is the father of Roger B. Chaffee, an astronaut on Apollo I, and who lives in the area. Chaffee read a letter his son had written to an eight year old who wanted to be an astronaut. "You have to want to dedicate your life to a worthwhile cause," Roger had written. Chaffee used the letter to convince his young audience that they, too, could become astronauts with the right combination of dedication, determination, training, and encouragement.

Chaffee understands the dedication part. In 1967 his son demonstrated the price of a dream. He died during tests when his Apollo I spacecraft caught fire. The elder Chaffee didn't skip over that in his talk.

Why does he spend time talking to students, especially such young ones?

Roger was a dreamer. He dreamed for things that were within the grasp of all mankind. Today's youth must learn to forecast life's directions and rates of change. They must be able to look twenty-five to fifty years into the future and see the human relationships that will prevail and the types of moral and ethical questions that may arise, and then they must have the technological ability to solve these problems.[5]

The technological ability comes later; the commitment begins now. Donald Chaffee, seventy-eight, is one of millions who are interested in the next generation of dreamers. America must reexamine its commitment to providing excellence at every stage of public education, from preschool through graduate school.

Every American school should be a place to dream, a place to test the dream, a place to refine that dream as one passes through the different educational levels. School should be a place to assemble the essential, nonnegotiable components of a dream:

- the ability to read;
- the ability to write;
- the ability to remedy what one does not know;
- the ability to communicate verbally;
- the ability to think critically.

Too many graduates of our high schools cannot perform at basic levels. We have long known of the book *Why Johnny Can't Read*. Yet despite the debates and increased expenditures, many Johnnys and Jills cannot read. And if they cannot read, they will have a tough time dreaming.

Much has been written lately about the sorry state of collegiate athletics, the football and basketball players who cannot read. One athlete is suing his high school for graduating him as an illiterate. Yet Georgetown University basketball coach John Thompson said of college athletes who flunk courses: "It wasn't a coach who passed these kids from grade 1 through 6 when they weren't able to read."[6]

As a dreamer, with or without school-age children, you need to be concerned about your local schoolboard's definition of excellence and its philosophy of the boundaries of a child's potential to learn.

**Interest Area 2: *Potential***

Take 100 randomly selected children born in 1986, who will be kindergarteners in 1991. Of these 100 future dreamers:

12 have been born to unmarried parents;

40 have been born to parents who will divorce before the child is 18;

5 have parents who will separate;

2 have been born to parents one of whom will die before the child is 18.

Only 41 of these 100 future dreamers will reach their eighteenth birthdays in intact, "traditional" families.[7] Increasingly, the change in the family unit influences schools' roles. Schools are almost forced to step in and fill the gap. Educators know that parental involvement is essential in students' achievement. However, consider the number of children in one-parent homes or whose mothers work full time. How can these mothers, who have an eight-hour job and are also managing a home, supervise homework with the same time and energy as mothers of an earlier generation, who stayed at home? The Japanese, however, insist on active parental involvement.

Look at H. Ross Perot, the Texas billionaire and entrepreneur, chairman of Electronic Data Systems, an Annapolis graduate who pioneered in the computer field. He, too, became interested in the next generation of dreamers and therefore accepted the appointment as chairman of the Texas Select Committee on Public Education, empowered to examine the quality of education in the state.

Perot believes that the ethnic groups and minorities are being shortchanged by the definitions of "potential" and "philosophy."

> We had a public school system that lived with a myth that every child in Texas came from a middle class family with a mother that didn't work, with two adoring parents, and if they didn't teach them anything at school the mother was somehow going to teach them that night anyway. If you didn't come from that sort of background, guess what we called you—uneducable![8]

As a result of Perot's involvement, the committee tackled tough issues and had the clout to persuade the state legislature to declare, "The purpose of the system is to develop *each child's* [and not just those who fit the myth] *full* potential" (italics mine). Perot added, "We had to change the school system for the world that exists" so that Texas children could be educated to compete in a real world.[9]

Perot, in his lecture at Vanderbilt University, insisted, "The only real legacy we can leave our children is a fully developed intellect and the ability to think." And Perot believes the ability to think is the ability to learn and to be able to adapt to new situations and change.[10]

Ninety-seven percent of Japanese students finish high school. In Chicago it's about 27 percent and half of those who do finish cannot read at a high-school level. The illiteracy rate in Japan is 1 percent, in the United States, it's 27 percent.[11]

### 3. BE INVOLVED WITH THE NEXT GENERATION OF DREAMERS

Dreamers cannot leave educational questions to experts and bureaucrats. All of us have a stake in the products of our public educational systems. Consider the enormous expenditures of federal, state, and local taxes that go to support them. Are we getting a good—let alone maximum—return on that investment?

Perot's involvement should be a model for others. Some men would have been too busy building their own dreams to undertake such a time-consuming enterprise. However, Ross Perot has an ability to understand and predict the future and perceives the need for an educated citizenry to cope with the challenges of living in the twenty-first century. He is not an elitist who wants the best for a few; he insists that in a democracy all must have the potential to dream, to explore their intellectual and creative endowment.

Many executives would not have had the stamina to return such a precedent-shattering report. Perot's committee convinced the Texas legislature to pass strong new laws that prevented students not passing academic courses from participating in sports or in extracurricular activities. There were howls of protest in the football-zealous state when huge numbers of athletes were ruled ineligible. Lawsuits were filed to test the legality of the committee's rules. Perot and his committee won.

Moreover, given the huge number of illegal aliens living in Texas, Perot fought for a redistribution of money among the rich and the poor school districts. He fought for literacy tests for teachers and a preschool program for culturally deprived and non-English-speaking children. Finally, Perot demanded a renewed emphasis on elementary education.

As a businessman, Perot demonstrated that Texas was spending $9 billion a year to be forty-fifth out of the fifty states in academic achievement, a poor return on the state's investment.[12] His was a heroic involvement.

In New York another entrepreneur, Eugene Lang, captured the attention of the media after he spoke in a "poverty-stricken, drug-ridden, despair-plagued" Harlem elementary school in June 1981. Lang, who had graduated from that school fifty-three years earlier, had been asked to give the graduation address for sixty-one sixth graders. He said:

> This is your *first* graduation—just the perfect time to dream. Dream of what you want to be, of the kind of life you wish to build. And believe in that dream. Be prepared to work for it. Always remember, each dream is important because it is *your* dream, it is *your* future. And it is worth working for.

The speaker paused, then resumed his text:

> You must study. You must learn. You must attend junior high school, high school and then college. You must go to college.

Some of the audience yawned; others were impatient to see the diplomas awarded. Lang's speech would have been far more appropriate on Long Island.

As he concluded, Eugene Lang added: "If you stay in school and graduate, I will give each of you a college scholarship."

No doubt some thought this was just a crazy, white man, not quite all there. But Eugene Lang put his words into writing giving each student a letter as a guarantee of his promise.[13]

Lang soon realized that these students needed someone who believed in them, someone to be in touch with them daily, if they were going to benefit from his generosity. So he hired John Rivera, a Harlem native, to coach and counsel the students.

Lang also created the I Have a Dream Foundation and invested $2,000 in the name of each student. Each year, he has added $2,000 to each student's account. The total will be sufficient to finance their educational dreams.

Why? Because Lang, who grew up in a Harlem tenement, who started his first business at age eight, who has done well in high tech, is a dreamer. Eugene Lang believes "that each individual soul is of infinite worth and infinite dignity." A zip code should be no barrier to an individual's potential to achieve. When students "have no purpose, they drift, unmotivated by dreams and hopes. Every trouble I can think of stems from individuals not being given the chance to set goals that will make them constructive, valuable members of society," Lang concluded.

Six years later, of the fifty-one who remained in New York, forty-eight have received their high school diplomas; twenty-four are in college, with sixteen more expected to enroll in the fall term, 1988. And Lang hasn't given up on the few dropouts.[14]

America has prided itself on access to its educational opportunities. Yet the cost of higher education has become enormous. The *Los Angeles Times* declared, "Without citizens with talent and skills to compete in a high tech world, the nation will pay in far more painful ways." The paper then blasted the proposed budget cuts of $3.7 billion that would reduce scholarships and work-study jobs:

> College isn't an inalienable right, but students should have
> an equal shot based on brains, not on ability or interest. It is in

the best interest of future generations of students and of this nation to help more—not fewer—Americans obtain a college education.[15]

This was the dream of Lyndon B. Johnson, who lobbied hard for the Higher Education Act of 1965, which made the federal government guarantor of access for many students. Johnson had to borrow money to attend Southwest Texas State College; now he wanted to provide funds to help students pursue their dreams. Moreover, the awareness of *Sputnik* and the shortage of math and science teachers helped to convince Congress to enact his dream.

I did not qualify for academic scholarships to attend college, but this federal money made me the first in my family to graduate from college. I also profited from the interest of two Louisianans, Ed and Gladys Hurley, whom I never met. Their trust fund paid the first two years of my graduate tuition.

I have an interest and a debt. I cannot sit by and let the government cut out funds for the next generation of dreamers. I have to write senators and congressmen, and I have to give to scholarship appeals.

I am a graduate of Vanderbilt University in Nashville, an expensive school to attend. In 1986 the university provided $16.5 million in student aid.[16] That student aid insures that many students will receive a Vanderbilt education who otherwise could not. While some students come to Vandy in private jets or in Porsches, others come by Greyhound. Each of them can become a freshman because the university believes that that student will be able to compete successfully in the academic program. Vanderbilt is not a revolving door.

The talent in each entering freshman class is incredible. Not all are academic superstars; but all are bright and energetic and enthusiastic dreamers. And there is a commitment to these students that, if they should stumble, the university will make extraordinary efforts to help them.

That's why groups of alumni stuff envelopes and use the phones for telethons—not just at Vanderbilt but at colleges and universities all across the nation. They are taking an interest in the next generation.

Another way of showing interest is through trusteeship. I became one of the youngest college trustees in this country and served thirteen years. I felt frustrated much of that time because my giving could not match that of several wealthy trustees, but I was always challenged to find those who could give at significant levels to Scarritt College.

However, most of the money that is raised for education in this country goes to colleges and universities. In 1984, 411 corporations contributed $562 million to education, but only $26 million went to precollege institutions and most of that was to secondary schools.[17] In an era of tax economy and budget cutbacks and cost-cutting, it's easy to assume there are plenty of tax dollars to go around. In my home city of Kansas City, citizens have voted down tax increases for schools four times. Across the country many school districts are financially impoverished.

Schools need dreamers, like Eugene Lang and Ross Perot, to invest their wealth and wisdom into educating the next generation of dreamers. You need to be interested in schools at all levels, not because they are in trouble but because education is essential in a democratic society committed to the freedom to dream.

I have to admit that I am a sucker for every student who knocks on my front door selling something to benefit his school. I buy tickets for chili suppers even though I will be a 1,000 miles away on that day. It is great for the child to learn to "sell" his school and to learn initiative, but it is also good citizenry on my part.

I live across the street from the Jane Hartman Elementary School. A couple of years ago I came home and found an invitation on my door for their open house for the neighborhood. Even though I do not have children and was scheduled to lecture in California, I arranged to come home a day early to attend that program.

I was stunned. I was the only neighbor who showed up.

As a writer, I am concerned that Hartman School prepare a generation of readers and critical thinkers. Are you, as a dreamer, involved? Could you find ways to be more involved? To get others involved?

## 4. BE OPEN TO CREATIVITY IN SPECIAL CHILDREN

The foundation for Children with Learning Disabilities ran this ad in *Time:*

Let No Child Be Demeaned, nor Have His Wonder Diminished, Because of Our Ignorance or Inactivity.

Let No Child Be Deprived of Discovery, Because We Lack the Resources to Discover His Problem.

Let No Child—Ever—Doubt Himself or His Mind Because We Are Unsure of His Commitment.[18]

Or because of our lack of excitement and enthusiasm. All children need to share the products of their learning and dreaming with interested, loving adults. Your enthusiasm must include those special children who once would have been called "retarded" or "handicapped," as well as the obviously gifted child or the normal child. Some of these individuals find the advantage in the word, dis*advantaged*.

Research on children termed "superkids," or "invulnerables," reveals that despite the stress in which these children live, they survive and thrive. Psychiatrist James E. Anthony has studied children of psychotic patients at Washington University Medical School in St. Louis. He was impressed by one poor, limping girl who responded kindly to him and put him at ease. He was stunned by her answer to his question, "What do you want to do when you grow up?" "I want to become a nurse and help look after poor children in India."

Many have assumed these children live in awful houses and have awful parents. Therefore, they expect awful results—self-fulfilling prophecies.

Not so, says Anthony and other researchers. In fact, the circumstances create within the children a tremendous need to overcome obstacles and an ability to cope with whatever life dishes out. Traditionally, researchers have looked for children who do not make it. Instead, Anthony has focused on those who have coped and are coping. He has identified several characteristics of the superkids. Socially, they seem exceptionally at ease and they make other people feel comfortable too. They know how to attract and use the support of adults.[19]

Carol Kaufman, of Massachusetts Mental Health Center, who studied competency of children of psychotic mothers, discovered, "The encouragement that such children obtain from teachers, relatives, baby-sitters, and other adults often plays a key role in their lives, making up for some of the support that their parents do not [cannot] give them."[20]

Despite their difficulties, these children actively try to master their environment and have some sense of their own power. They think for themselves and develop a high degree of autonomy. They are achievers and generally do well at most things they attempt.

Superkids have an ability to carve out "a little private place" for themselves somewhere in their environment. One boy, according to Anthony, retreated to his basement where he had created an intellectual oasis with a stereo and books. Superkids have an ability to put up not only physical distance but also psychological distance.

One boy, whose parents were psychotic, retreated into the world of creative writing; he even wrote a novella about his family. Then he went on to write plays and, at last report, was working as an actor and director in the theater.

Dreamers need to be enthusiastic about such children, regardless of their ages, for these children, with the help of a dreamer, will be able to disprove the cultural notion "like father, like son."

### 5. BE TOUGH

Children need more than pats on the head. Indeed, Dr. Susan Littwin, in her book *The Postponed Generation,* insisted that we have often been too quick to praise, so much so that there is now a generation of young adults who are postponing the responsibilities and autonomy of adulthood. This generation was brought up in "playpens ringed by safety nets" and thus has a fear of failing.[21]

Littwin questions the young adults who work years as waiters or waitresses, taking courses, trying to find themselves. Many have "escapist creativity" and pass themselves as artists or musicians but do not earn a living from their skills. Instead, they are subsidized by Mom and Dad. Their talent is a "great attention getter. It allows them to be admired, dependent children forever. And that course feeds itself. If you assume responsibility for your talent and produce, you run the risk of not being as good as your potential" (and you also run the risk of starving).[22]

Littwin further noted "there are so many of them because so many were special, identified as talented, and encouraged to pursue their talents. Like the super students, they were given a sense of destiny, but no one ever told them that achieving that destiny would require sacrifice and risk."[23] Avoidance of risk thwarts their dreams.

What about those who have seen their "hot" fields go stale; such as those who earned degrees in geology—like my bug man find themselves in debt, or find themselves doing some boring job "in the meantime"?

Ross Perot worries about the future for children. "We stand the chance of being the first generation not to leave our children a better life."[24]

Littwin added, "Today's college student leaves campus to find that the life-style he grew up with is not waiting at the corner for him. The economy has shrunk, his college class is large, and jobs are hard to get. If his parents' house were on the market, he wouldn't be able to afford it."[25]

The tough challenge, according to Perot, is to prepare our children to live in an age of information; to live in an age when change occurs very rapidly; to live in an age when many of them will work at least five unrelated jobs in their lifetimes.

That's why we have to be tough and teach them to be tough and resourceful. We will have to design curriculums to be more than smorgasbords of courses, "a taste of this, a smattering of that."[26]

Dreamers will have to be computer literate.

Dreamers will need to be readers (that means we have to start them reading early and provide library cards).

Dreamers will have to have an American perspective. We are a racial and ethnic hodgepodge. The celebration for the 100th anniversary of the Statue of Liberty proved that. Yet now, a new wave of immigration from Mexico and Central America and from Asia will challenge us. The newcomers will bring much from their cultures, as they search for that "golden door" that has beckoned so many others.

We are rich; we are poor. Yet, as Bennett says, "the persistence of a socioeconomic underclass in American society looms as one of the largest challenges to our nation in general and to our education system in particular."[27]

As I write this, there has been an eruption of racism in Howard Beach, New York, and in Forsyth, Georgia. Suddenly, students are confronted with something they had only read about in history books: racism. How will this generation deal with racism?

Dreamers need a global perspective. The world is shrinking. Computers have a global language. *Newsweek* recently had a cover story: "Your Next Employer May Be Japanese." That would have been thought impossible a few years ago, and the idea sends shock waves through Detroit. A dreamer's colleague may be someone not only in the next lab or down the hall or across campus . . . but also across the world.

Dreamers need a sense of individual responsibility. They need to realize that dreaming is a continuum, that each of us must take part in keeping alive that commitment to dreaming. Thus, if we are tough, we will see schools as places to dream. We will also see teachers as dream educators. We will see a significant function of the school to be to develop an appreciation for dreams.

One of the great experiments along this line is taking place in the Syracuse, New York, public schools. A large number of the 33,000 students were considered "at risk" students. But civic leaders have chosen to alter the system radically to turn out students who can read, write, compute, use technology, and be ready for the workplace. Said Kay Whitmore, the president of Kodak, which employs 45,000 in the city, "If we don't improve the quality of the students in our city school system, we're [meaning Eastman Kodak] in trouble."[28]

Change began when five men committed to meet regularly for breakfast: Kay Whitmore; Peter McWalters, superintendent of schools; Adam Urbanski, head of the Rochester teacher's association; Bill Johnson, head of the Urban League; and Dennis O'Brien, president of the University of Rochester.

McWalters, armed with notebooks full of grim statistics, convinced the group over the eggs and bacon that "It's not a question of doing it harder. It's a question of doing it differently," of producing results. Soon they realized that McWalters was not offering a quick fix for what ailed the schools but a long-term solution. Whitmore added, "The best way to enhance quality is to get it right the first time."[29]

The men organized a business industry task force, through which five executives spent a year studying the school system and those in other cities. That led to the Rochester Brainpower Program, which resulted in an effective ad campaign, partnerships between schools and businesses, and the placement of a company-paid job counselor in every school.

Many consider the plan a high stakes, ($31 million cost) gamble. Others insist Rochester will become a model for the nation's 15,000 school districts. The program is not just for window dressing or for selected students. McWalters vows, "Student performance is the only means of evaluation I will accept. And not just for some students. All students."[30]

What is happening in Rochester *could happen* in your school district. When dreamers work together, amazing things can happen. The tough challenge is to make sure that students leave schools prepared to take charge of their own destinies, equipped to pursue their dreams. They must be encouraged to manage the processes, with the inevitable ups and downs, right turns, left turns, and detours.

## 6. BE REALISTIC

The problems of American education will not be solved by throwing a few more billion dollars at the schools. Indeed, Bennett claims that our schools do not lack money. Instead, they struggle with a combination of confusion, bureaucratic thinking, and apathy.

The equipping of the next generation of dreamers requires fresh involvement and fresh approaches. If schools cannot make room in their designs for dreaming, then a thousand dream places must be created that will stimulate the next generation. Whether after school, during the summers, or in alternative settings, the next generation must be challenged to dream and to embrace its own dream.

Each child needs at least one person who genuinely cares. Thus, we need thousands of Ross Perots and Eugene Langs and Kay Whitmores—at least one or two in every school district in America—who actively encourage the next generation to dream.

Every day after lunch in the fourth grade, my teacher, Mrs. Alice Cannon, read the great legends of Paul Bunyan, a lumberjack. I loved to hear those stories. I wonder why we can't develop stories of our heroes, our dreamers, our entrepreneurs.

Maybe that will be the lasting legacy of Christa McAuliffe, the first teacher in space. Although she never gave the lesson she had scheduled to teach from space, her life was a lesson, the lesson of a dreamer.

Not all legends are dramatic. Some are ordinary, if not common. But each is like a piece of a puzzle.

The next generation deserves our best. The big question is how Americans will perceive the cost of educating the next generation of dreamers: as a cost or as an investment?

Not all families or schools nurture future dreamers. I think of a young boy who was told "day in, day out, I looked like a freak, had the mind of an idiot, and would die in the gutter if not in the electric chair." Pretty tough words, huh? Imagine the impact on a six year old.

Somehow his childish dream survived the cruel blows of reality. Fortunately, he had a grandmother who loved him without "stint and with no strings attached, who helped him survive with some degree of sanity those dreadful years of childhood." When she died, an art teacher took her place.[31]

Today this young dreamer's art is exhibited in major museums and significant collections around the world. He has the distinction of being the first living American artist to have had a one-man show at the Metropolitan Museum in New York City. The events of his life, "some welcomed, others endured," shaped the young man into Jules Olitski.

Olitski's work reminds me of the words of Lyndon Johnson to a group of educators: "We just must not, we just cannot afford the great waste that comes from the neglect of a single child."

~~~~~~~~~~~~~~~~~~~~

1. How acquainted are you with children of today?

   ____ Not at all
   ____ Somewhat
   ____ Very much so

2. Did you find the statistics quoted on pp. 149–153 surprising? Disturbing? In what way?

3. How active are you with today's children and teens?

4. Do the Japanese have a valid point in arguing "All children can learn" and thereby structuring their

educational system accordingly? Or do you prefer
the American philosophy?

5. Is there a happy medium between the two philosophies?

6. What do you think motivated Ross Perot to get involved
in public education?

7. Should you be as interested?

8. Although you may not be as rich as Eugene Lang, what
could you do to help disadvantaged children to dream?

9. What would it take to get your company or business
to invest in elementary and secondary education?

10. Why does a child need a "global" perspective when there
are so many problems at home?

11. In your judgment, what does a child need for survival
in our world?

12. Assuming that you do not have children, or
school-aged children, what are your obligations
to the next generation of dreamers?

# 11

## STEP TEN

# SAY YES TO THE DREAM

A father on a business trip discovered that his plane was going to be several hours late. In the days before credit card phone calling, he called home to tell his wife. However, she was not at home, and his eight-year-old son answered. "I have a collect call from Jim Hawkins. Will you accept the charges?"

"He's not here," the eight year old announced.

"They won't accept the charges," the operator matter-of-factly reported.

"I'm Jim Hawkins," the man reported. Over the line he again heard, "He's not here."

Once again the operator tried to ask if the little boy's mother was "there." Again she asked if anyone would accept a collect call from Jim Hawkins.

"He's not here," the eight year old again repeated.

In frustration, the father said, "Jimmy, just say yes."

Jimmy did and the call went through.

Perhaps you've heard the Southern evangelist who frequently shouts to his audience, "Say YESSS!" That's what I would hope you would say to your dream. You may not enthusiastically yell YES! like a cheerleader at a pep rally. You may, in a quiet moment, whisper your yes. But your dream deserves a yes. And the world needs your dream.

A quick reading of the morning newspaper or thirty minutes with Dan Rather or Tom Brokaw reminds one that there couldn't be a better time than now for dreamers. We need dreamers young and old, married and single, male and female, educated and unlettered, charismatic and reserved. We need dreamers who will dare to make a difference for the good.

Someone sent me a card for my fortieth birthday with these words on the outside, "If the Lord hadn't wanted us to reach for the stars . . ." and on the inside, "He wouldn't have blessed us with the power to dream." I believe that.

In my files I have an advertisement for PF Flyers shoes by Converse. It shows a little blond-haired boy mimicking the pose of the classic sculpture "The Discus Thrower." The copy line reads, "Many champions are born and then unmade."[1] I wonder if the same cannot be said of dreamers: Many *dreamers* are born . . . then unmade.

You've read this book. Now what are you going to do with what you've read? Several times you have identified with a particular dreamer whose story I've told. You have underlined sentences that leaped out to you, for they echoed words you have heard yourself say. You've thought, *That sounds like me*.

This book has been an invitation to join a long line of dreamers who persisted until they found the hope in *hope*lessness and the help in *help*lessness. Dreams have no magnitudinal dimension. A small dream is still a worthy dream. The same principles apply for all dreams, big, small, or in-between-size.

In 1948 a young minister went to California to speak at a conference for college students in the San Bernardino mountains near Los Angeles. He had been invited by Henrietta Mears, who loved to encourage dreamers. She had been criticized for inviting this young man because he was immature, was considered unorthodox, and wasn't from an established church. Miss Mears stood firm.

The young man was struggling with his dream and also with his desire to do doctoral work in England. Yet his deeper struggle was with Scripture. Could he believe that the Bible was true in light of seeming contradictions? Could he believe that the Bible was true in light of today's problems and needs and realities? In June 1948 he had held a ten-day meeting in Altoona,

Pennsylvania. His associates labeled it "The greatest flop we've ever had anywhere." While the young man could have blamed poor preparation and tension between the pastors of local congregations, he believed the failure lay in his nagging uncertainty. Maybe his good friend Charles Templeton was right when he said, "Your faith is too simple. You'll have to get a new jargon if you want to communicate to *this* generation."[2]

At Miss Mears's college conference, the young minister spoke brilliantly in the mornings, but in the afternoons and early evenings he often sat by a fishpond with Dr. Edwin Orr and confessed his intellectual struggle and doubts.

One afternoon the young minister heard repeated what Templeton had said earlier that morning: "Poor _____. If he goes on the way he's going, he'll never do anything for God. He'll be circumscribed to a small, little, narrow interpretation of the Bible, and his ministry will be curtailed. As for me, I'm taking a different road."

The remark, even though taken out of context, wounded the young man. Instead of attending the evening session, he wandered the mountain trails asking, "Lord, what shall I do? What shall be the direction of my life?" That summer night he faced the ultimate crossroad as he thought through the questions that had been bothering him. He realized that intellect couldn't resolve all of them. Finally, he placed his Bible on a stump and knelt on the ground. He continued to wrestle with those questions until he made a decision.

"Oh God," he prayed, "I cannot prove certain things. I cannot answer some of the questions Chuck is raising and some of the other people are raising, but I accept this book by faith as the Word of God."[3]

The young minister came down from that mountain and walked into history. His name: William Franklin ("Billy") Graham.

What if he had thrown in the towel in Altoona, Pennsylvania? What if he had thrown in the towel along one of those mountain trails? What if he had not said yes? What if?

That could be said of you someday.

## SAY YES TO THE INVITATION TO DREAM

In chapter 7 I shared the story of Abraham. Now let me share the story of his great-grandson, Joseph, Jacob's favorite son. Joseph could do no wrong. But his brothers dismissed him as "the dreamer." They hated him and could not speak "peaceably to him" because they realized that their aging father loved him more.[4]

Joseph had a dream, and he "shared" it with his brothers. (Sometimes dreamers have been known to be cursed with a chronic poor sense of timing.) He then had a second dream, which produced more outrage in his brothers, because Joseph had dreamed that he would someday rule over them.

One day Jacob sent Joseph to see how his other sons were doing grazing sheep in the Hebron Valley. When his brothers saw him at a distance, they "conspired . . . to kill him."

How many times has that plot been carried out? If you don't like the dream, get rid of the dreamer?

So the brothers plotted to kill Joseph, dump the body into some pit, and tell their father, "some wild beast has devoured him." The plot made sense to them. One of the brothers arrogantly quipped, *"We shall see what will become of his dreams!"*[5]

Fortunately, one of the eleven had brains and a heart. Reuben talked them out of killing Joseph and into selling him to a caravan of traders. On the surface that doesn't seem too compassionate, but at least his life was spared.

The next chapters of Genesis read like the resume of some contemporary dreamers: ups and downs, right turns, left turns, U-turns. Your dream may not seem much of an invitation. But it is an opportunity, a beginning point.

## SAY YES, EVEN TO THE PIT

A pit is hardly the place to launch a dream, especially a dream as lofty as Joseph's. How could he rule over his brothers when he was in a dark hole? Clearly, they had put him in his place. What would become of his dream?

Yet dreamers say yes, even in the pit. In 1848 nine young Irish men were tried and convicted of treason against the British Crown: Thomas Francis Meagher, Terrence McManus, Patrick Donahue, Richard O'Gorman, Morris Lyene, Michael Ireland, Thomas D'Arcy McGee, John Mitchell, and Charles Duffy.

Before passing the sentence, the judge asked if anyone had anything to say. "Yes," said the red-haired, hot-blooded Meagher. "My lord, this is our first offense but not our last. If you will be easy with us this once, we promise, on our word as gentlemen, to try to do better next time."

That sounded logical. But Meagher should have stopped while he was ahead. "And next time, we won't be fools and get caught."

That was all the judge needed to hear. He sentenced them to be hanged, then drawn and quartered. He would teach the Irish rebels a lesson. Their sentences captured the attention of the world. Queen Victoria reluctantly bowed to the pressure of public opinion, and commuted their sentences to transportation to Australia.[6]

### Pits Can Be Valuable

Australia was then England's penal colony. The passage to Australia might kill the rebels, for although food was in short supply, disease and beatings were not. Moreover, trying to survive from the soil often proved an impossible sentence for city dwellers.

That was the end of them, Victoria thought. However, these nine men found their pit, Australia, a launching point. Years passed. When the Queen was informed in 1874 that Sir Charles Duffy had been elected prime minister of Australia, the name jogged her memory. Surely that was not the same man whose life she had spared. She launched an investigation and found that not only was Duffy the same the but the others had prospered also:

Thomas Francis Meagher had become governor of Montana;

Terrence McManus and Patrick Donahue, brigadier generals in the United States army;

Richard O'Gorman, governor general of Newfoundland;

Morris Lyene, attorney general of Australia, later succeeded
by Michael Ireland;

Thomas D'Arcy McGee, member of the Canadian Parlia-
ment and former minister of Agriculture;

John Mitchell, prominent New York City politician.[7]

The men said yes to a dream in a desperate environment, and
their dreams came true.

## Detours Can Be Bridges

One cartoon strip called "Big George" illustrated this principle. Big George was walking along a cliff, leading a donkey,
when he came to a point where the trail had collapsed creating
a chasm. Someone had erected a sign that said Detour.

Big George looked around. Detour? Where? A sheer drop
was below him; a solid wall of rock, straight up, above him. His
alternative: turn around and go back the way he had come.

Instead, Big George pulled up the detour sign, placed it
across the chasm, and used "Detour" as a bridge.

Often, successful adapters, like these Irishmen, are able to
turn detours into bridges to make dreams into reality. That still
makes sense. Use the detour as a bridge between where you are
now and where you want to go. Be creative with the detours en
route to your dream. And remember, the distance between you
and your dream is never as great as it seems.

## Rock Bottom May Be Valuable

Sometimes, you have to hit rock bottom, the pit. Jim Dycus
knows all about that. As a Chicago teen, dropping pills and
getting high was a way of life for him. Jim tried every drug he
could get his hands on. His addiction led him to a life of crime
to support his habit. In his own words, "Drugs consumed me. I
lived to put that needle in my arm, lived to feel that rush. Whatever I had to do to get that fix, I did it." He went in and out of
marriages, in and out of jail, despite his mother's, "Someday
you'll be sorry, Jimmy, someday . . ."

By 1970, Jim Dycus had lost everything that had ever meant
anything to him: family, children, jobs, respect. When he was

shot during a drug store robbery by Chicago police, he heard a policeman say over him, "Call the wagon on this scum!" After serving his sentence, he stumbled into Teen Challenge. He had hit rock bottom.[8]

Today, the Reverend Jim Dycus is minister with single adults at 10,000-member Calvary Assembly in Winter Park, Florida. Jim and his wife, Barb, have developed a curriculum for children of single-parent families, and he has authored several books and is a popular speaker. His biography, *Not Guilty*, was published by Harper and Row. Jim Dycus hit rock bottom and survived. A lot of people hit rock bottom. It's a question of what do you do then? Stay there and get worse, or change?

## Joseph Hit Rock Bottom Too

Joseph was sold to a caravan of traders and taken to Egypt. Eventually, he found himself a servant in the household of Potiphar, Pharaoh's captain of the guard. Considering the other assignments he could have had as a slave, he was doing well. In fact, everything he did prospered. Eventually, he worked his way up to overseer, and Potiphar left everything up to Joseph. That's when the trouble began.

Apparently, Joseph was good-looking, and Mrs. Potiphar "cast longing eyes" at Joseph. He recognized his predicament but refused to become sexually involved with her. Mrs. Potiphar would not be rejected, however. She attempted to seduce Joseph, then lied and accused Joseph of attempting to rape her.

Joseph's upward mobility took a sudden U-turn. He found himself in prison, though not just your run-of-the-mill prison. He ended up in the section with the king's prisoners. The bad news was that he was in prison; the good news was that again his life had been spared, this time by an irate husband.

Look at Joseph's resume: position of status to pit, to position of status to prison. Not a pretty picture. He had had two strikes against him in life; good thing he didn't know that with three strikes, you're out. What about his dream to rule, now?

Dreamers never waste experiences, even in prison. Joseph

worked. Again, even in prison, "*the* LORD *was with him; and whatever he did, the* LORD *made it prosper.*"[9]

Three thousand years later another Jewish man faced a struggle and used his experience to fulfill his dream. When World War II broke out, Aharon Appelfeld was an eight-year-old boy; his parents were thirty. When Nazis marched into his hometown of Czernovitz, Rumania, his mother was killed, and Aharon and his father became separated while being deported to a concentration camp. Quickly, this eight year old learned that his Jewishness was a death sentence.

One night however, he crawled under a fence and escaped. Appelfeld later claimed it was the reflex of a child facing death. After all, inside that camp, the only certainty was death.

*Surely someone would take me in,* he thought to himself. He quickly learned that the Ukrainian peasants would not jeopardize their lives to hide a Jew. So for three years Aharon wandered. Some middle-class people offered to take him in, but he realized their insistence on cleanliness and bathing might create a moment when the physical evidence of his Jewishness would be discovered.

So he slept in barns. He kept company with "marginal" types—prostitutes, horse thieves, fortune tellers—people who didn't ask many questions. For another three years he wandered until he was liberated by a Russian army unit. Eventually, he met up with a group of Jewish boys who had also survived the Holocaust by their wits. In 1945 he was sent to Israel, where again he did not fit in.

These experiences, however, these detours, shaped his mind. He wrote about his parents and his life on the run. The first publisher who read his manuscript said, "Well, you can certainly write—that's for sure. But why waste your talents preserving memories like these? What's the use of keeping them alive?"

Aharon Appelfeld had said yes to life and yes to his dream to write. He turned to another publisher, and soon his words were being warmly received by readers around the world. *Badenheim 1939, Land of Cattails, Age of Wonders, The Immortal Bart-*

*fuss* have made him one of Israel's greatest novelists. And now his work is gaining recognition in America.[10]

## SAY YES TO THE REJECTIONS

Aharon Appelfeld looked to prostitutes and others to help him survive. Joseph also looked to others for help. The dreamer is always figuring angles. One day Joseph interpreted the dreams of two fellow prisoners, Pharaoh's former chief cupbearer and his chief baker. The cupbearer's dream meant that he would be restored to his former position of favor with the king, Joseph said. In return for the interpretation, Joseph created something of an IOU: "But remember me when it is well with you, and please show kindness to me; make mention of me to Pharaoh, and get me out of this house."[11] (He was diplomatic in his description. The fact was he was in jail.)

Let's face it, the cupbearer could have and should have helped Joseph. But he didn't. That's life, as thousands of readers can testify from personal experience. The cupbearer wanted to forget his prison experience.

Two years passed. Two long years in a prison is tough on any dreamer. It might have been easy for Joseph to have sworn revenge. "Just wait 'til I get out of here." Or "If it's the last thing I ever do, I'll get that cupbearer." But revenge wastes energy. Revenge refuse to share quarters with a dream. It demands the mind and the heart of a person. Some dreamers have allowed it a small room; and in time, it controls two rooms, then three.

It's possible to invest all your eggs in one basket, to believe this promotion, this opportunity, this chance is *the* one. Yet things don't always work out.

In 1941 a young man, fresh out of Yale Law School, applied for acceptance as a special agent with the FBI. He was turned down by Director J. Edgar Hoover because the man's family might possibly be "subversive." The background check showed that the man's mother, though a Republican and the wife of the mayor of Cincinnati, Ohio, was a member of the League of Women Voters and the Peace League, a mildly antiwar group. Hoover drafted a memo and placed it with the application.

"Particular care [should] be given to the possibility that the applicant or his family may be engaged in subversive activities."

. The young man, though disappointed, launched into a legal career that eventually led to his appointment on the United States Supreme Court in 1958. Potter Stewart served the court for twenty-three years. Later he was appointed by President Reagan to serve on blue-ribbon commissions on organized crime and Central American policy.

He might have ended up with an FBI pension, but Justice Potter Stewart had an unquestioned career as a lawyer and a jurist. He accepted one rejection as the motivation to try another.[12]

### SAY YES TO THE ADVENTURE

When Pharaoh had a dream that none of the wise men or magicians in Egypt could interpret, the chief cupbearer "suddenly" remembered his former cellmate, Joseph. Immediately, Joseph got a shave, bath, and change of clothing and found himself eyeballing none other than the Pharaoh.

Joseph listened, then interpreted the dream, concluding, "Let Pharaoh select a discerning and wise man, and set him over the land of Egypt" (in light of a bad famine that was coming).[13] I don't believe Joseph saw any connection to his dream. After all, he'd been out of the cell block for half an hour. The best he was hoping for was probably a good meal.

Obviously, there was a shortage of wise men in Egypt then. Moments later, Joseph couldn't believe his ears: "You shall be over my house, and all my people shall be ruled according to your word."[14]

The next thing the dreamer knew he had Pharaoh's signet ring on his finger; he had fine linen garments and a gold chain around his neck. His mind must have been swirling with the rapid turn of events. But the adventure of saving Egypt from the ravage of a famine captured his imagination.

Surely his brothers back in the Hebron must have occasionally wondered about whatever happened to Joseph.

In the 1930s a newspaper editor became concerned about one of his sportswriters. He never seemed to produce. Time and again the editor warned the writer about his lack of imagination in his writing. "If you would quit doodling and concentrate, you might make something of yourself." Eventually, he fired the sportswriter. But that firing began the great adventure for Walt Disney. Now he was free to give all his time to his cartoon friends, Mickey and Minnie Mouse and Donald Duck. His dream began with a good idea.

His cartoon strips were widely read. Soon, his characters came to life in the movies, and later, in television. Walt Disney was a man who possessed and was possessed by a dream.

As a child, I remember watching the Mouseketeers Club each afternoon. Sunday nights were Disney nights; week after week, the dreamer and his craftsmen introduced children to Fantasyland, Adventureland, Frontierland, and Tomorrowland. His theme song found its way to a generation of children: "When you wish upon a star, / Makes no difference who you are."

A generation of children believed that. And those children had parents who believed in giving them the opportunities they, the parents, had missed.

Disney never stopped dreaming. In the forties, small amusement parks with thrill rides were built in large cities. When Disney and his daughters visited them, he discovered they were "dirty, phoney places, run by tough-looking people." Disney said, "There was a need for something new, but I didn't know what it was."[15]

Moreover, on those Saturday outings with his daughters, he noticed that while the girls rode the merry-go-round, he sat on a bench, eating peanuts, feeling very alone. There ought to be a way, he thought, for parents and children to do things together.

So he began to dream and to sketch and to share his ideas with associates. The amusement park he dreamed of would be the world's biggest toy for the world's biggest boy.

As he talked with the manufacturers of rides, they wanted to sell him their standard fare. They could not comprehend Disney's ideas. Even his brother Roy dismissed the idea as "another of Walt's screwy ideas." Amusement park owners thought Disney should stick to cartoons, movies, and television.

Slowly the dream moved from sketches to blueprints. Now

Disney launched stage two: trying to raise the money to build his dream—an estimated $17 million. Bankers lectured him that the outdoor amusement parks were a cultural anachronism, going the way of the dinosaur. The few who actually looked at the Disney plans, shook their heads in dismay. Forget it, they said.

Finally, Disney tapped into his own life insurance for money to keep the dream alive. Slowly, here and there, he found risk takers for a project called Disneyland. The rest is history.[16]

Why? Because a man said yes to the adventure.

Or consider a six-foot-two insurance salesman in Owings, Maryland. Severe myopia, requiring eyeglasses so thick they resembled Coke-bottle bottoms, kept him out of the military. Still, he read military literature and took ROTC courses at Loyola College, where he majored in English. When he graduated, he took the first job that was offered: selling insurance.

Since high-school days he had dreamed of writing a novel. Three events over a seven year period influenced him to start: hearing about the 1975 attempted defection of a Russian submarine to Sweden; having lunch with a submariner; and reading a thesis about the 1975 event.

In 1982 Tom Clancy devoured *Combat Fleets of the World* and *Guide to the Soviet Navy*. Then for seven months he hammered away at his typewriter on a novel he called *Red October*. He sold it to the Naval Institute Press. How many people would want to read a novel about the Soviet navy? No romance, no sex; just water.

But Clancy had the capacity to write action scenes that grabbed readers by the jugular. Then President Reagan read it and called it "a perfect yarn." Overnight, *Red October,* by an unknown insurance salesman, was on the *New York Times* best-seller list, where it remained for twenty-nine weeks. Since then, Clancy has dined with the president, assorted admirals, toured submarines, and driven M–1 tanks. His sequels, *Red Storm Rising* and *Patriot Games,* have been best sellers too.[17]

Why? Tom Clancy, like Walt Disney, like thousands of others, said yes to the dream. And they all said yes to the price the dream demanded.

## SAY YES TO MAKING A DIFFERENCE

A terrific famine in the land forced Joseph's brothers to go to Egypt to buy grain from their brother, who remained incognito. Remember, the last time they had seen their brother he was on the back of a camel heading to Egypt. If he had been awake, he might have had revenge in his eyes—"If it is the last thing I ever do, I'll get you for this!"—or perhaps an incredible pleading—"Please, don't do this to me!"

In one of the most heart-rending scenes in the Old Testament, when the brothers had finished negotiating a grain purchase, Joseph ordered all the Egyptians out of the room. What a moment to get them back for all their wrongs. Instead, he announced, "I am Joseph!" The brothers could not answer him; they were terrified (and rightly so).

But Joseph said, "Come near to me. . . . I am Joseph your brother, whom you sold into Egypt. But now, do not therefore be grieved nor angry with yourselves because you sold me here; for God sent me before you to preserve life."[18]

Joseph, like many dreamers, could see God's hand working in the midst of the mess. As Sören Kierkegaard observed, "Life can only be lived forwards but it can only be understood backwards." Now they understood the dream they had thought terminated in the pit. Then the dreamer "kissed all his brothers and wept over them."[19]

Names were important to ancient peoples. What Joseph chose to name his two sons provides insight into this dreamer's heart. He named his firstborn, *Manasseh,* "for God has made me forget all my toil and my father's house."[20] This dreamer hadn't sat around plotting revenge; he had saved Egypt from famine. His second son he named *Ephraim,* "for God has caused me to be fruitful in the land of my affliction."[21]

That's the ultimate test for the dreamer. If God made Joseph "fruitful" in the land of his suffering, could he not do the same for you?

After writing this book, I am convinced of one thing: We do not read or think our way into our dream—we leap. And sometimes that leap seems totally outrageous to our family, friends, and colleagues. That leap may prompt a "have you lost your mind?" Yet God never said we would be leading at half-time. Sometimes, as in athletics, we need an overtime or extra innings. So it is with the dream.

I have asked you
to evaluate your dream;
to avoid the rainchecks;
to pick your dream turf;
to dare to launch your dream;
to communicate your dream to others;
to have faith in yourself and your dream;
to learn to restore the dream;
to balance the dream;
to nurture the next generation of dreamers;
and most importantly, to say yes.

You can follow all the steps; you can enjoy the book, even share it with others; but if you do not say yes to your dream, the world will have missed something special.

As I browsed in a used book store in Sarasota, Florida, I found a copy of Ralph De Toledano's *RFK: The Man Who Would Be President,* a biography of Robert Kennedy. De Toledano wrote the book in 1967 when many politicians were expecting Kennedy to challenge the incumbent, Lyndon Johnson. Less than a year later, the night after he won the California primary, Kennedy was shot in the kitchen of a Los Angeles hotel. The dream ended short of the nomination.

De Toledano could find no magic moment when Kennedy decided to run. In his life there had been thousands of hurdles, small and large, which had shaped the decision. But none moreso than the small silver box his brother John had given Bobby after the successful 1960 campaign. JFK had had it inscribed, *"When I'm Through, How About You?"*[22]

Would Robert have ever run if his brother had not opened the door? That ties in to what Mary Bethune, college president and later counselor to President Franklin D. Roosevelt, said of her life. Many women said that if Mrs. Bethune could just get into the doorway, "She will stand and hold it open so that other women may pass through."[23]

Mary Bethune said the "glory" of her dream was not being president of a college, counselor to a president, head of a great women's federation, but being a doorkeeper. "I must open the doors to fuller life—I must open many of them—as I pass this way, . . . for the people who come after me."[24]

Comedian Steve Allen was right when he observed, "The deity has never yet miraculously introduced into the human drama a hospital, orphanage, convent, church, synagogue, temple, cancer research institute, or any other helpful social institution. He leaves that to the more compassionate of his creatures."[25] To the dreamers.

I hope that you, as a dreamer, will be a bridge over which others may reach their dreams. And that you will take your rightful place in a great cadre of dreamers who have dared to improve this world under the smile of God.

I have tried to explain dreaming in such a way that someone, by reading *No Fear of Trying*, will put the book down and say yes.

Now that I am through, what about you? What will you do with the precious gift called a dream? There has never been a better moment than now to launch a dream.

There has never been a better moment than now to recommit yourself to your dream.

There has never been a better moment than now to say yes.

Wherever you are on your dream path, whatever your age, my closing thought to you is: Dreams become reality for people who have no fear of trying.

~~~~~~~~~~~~~~~~~~~~~~~~~

1. Has a detour ever been beneficial to you?

2. What has been the impact of "rock bottom" on you?

3. What holds you back from saying an enthusiastic yes to your dream?

4.  If you cannot say yes to your dream now, do you envision a time when you can?

5.  How could your dream be a doorway for other dreams?

6.  Will there ever be a better time than now to say yes?

~~~~~~~

THERE MAY WELL BE
THAT MOMENT
WHEN I CONCLUDE
   MY DREAM
   IS UNREACHABLE
   AND I GIVE UP.
ALL I KNOW IS
   IT WON'T BE TODAY.
—Harold Ivan Smith

~~~~~~~

# NOTES

## Chapter 1

1. "Longwood" (Natchez, Mississippi: Pilgrimage Garden Club).
2. Mario M. Cuomo, "The American Dream and the Politics of Inclusion," *Psychology Today,* July 1986, 54.
3. "Vermont Governor Urges Women to Run," *USA Today,* August 21, 1987, 2A.
4. Jim Stewart, "Navy's Sleeping Giants Awaken to a New World," *Atlanta Constitution,* May 26, 1987, 1-A.
5. Joseph J. Fucini and Suzy Fucini, *Entrepreneurs: The Men and Women Behind Famous Brand Names and How They Made It* (Boston: G. K. Hall, 1985), 82–84.
6. Kathleen Walker, "The Plastic Security Blanket," *World Vision,* October-November 1985, 22.
7. *Ibid.*
8. Mary Rowland, "Tales of Triumph," *Working Woman,* February 1988, 76. See also "Hallmark Card Ban Is Upheld," *Kansas City Times,* May 25, 1988, D-1.
9. *Ibid.,* 77–78.
10. "Longwood."
11. Irwin Ross, "Mr. Walkman Talks," *Fortune,* October 27, 1986, 143–144.
12. "AFA Cadet Travels Road from Refugee to Rhodes Scholar," *Colorado Springs Gazette-Telegraph,* December 8, 1986, B-1.
13. Esther 4:14.

## Chapter 2

1. Luke 14:28–29.
2. Meredith Tax, *Rievington Street* (New York: William Morrow, 1982), 208–209.

3. Jim Calio, "A New Plus for Safety, Ralph Baker's Life Chute May Save Lives in High-Rise Fires," *Illustrated People,* July 13, 1987, 107–108.

4. Peter Rinearson, "Piano Forte," *Seattle Times,* November 30, 1986, J–1.

5. Philippians 4:8.

6. Katherine DuPre Lumpkin, *The Emancipation of Angelina Grimké* (Chapel Hill: University of North Carolina, 1974), 146, 141; Janey Stevenson, "A Family Divided," *American Heritage,* 18 (April 1967), 4–8.

7. Gerda Lerner, *The Grimké Sisters from South Carolina* (New York: Schocken, 1971), 8–9, 10.

8. *Ibid.,* 266.

9. James Newton, *Uncommon Friends* (New York: Harcourt, Brace and Jovonovich, 1987), 9.

10. *Ibid.,* 9–10.

11. *Ibid.,* 11–12.

12. *Ibid.,* 20.

13. Robert V. Bruce, *Bell: Alexander Graham Bell and the Conquest of Solitude* (Boston: Little, Brown, 1973), 143.

14. "President Joins Nation in Mourning," *Orlando Sentinel,* January 20, 1986, A–5.

15. Matthew 16:26.

## Chapter 3

1. Esther 4:14.

2. Malcolm McConnell, *Challenger: A Major Malfunction* (Garden City: Doubleday, 1987), 196; "Challenger's Last Flight: A Special Report," *Los Angeles Times,* February 9, 1986, Part I-A, 1.

3. 1 Samuel 13:8–14.

4. "Up from the Deep," *Economist,* August 3, 1985, 22.

5. Montgomery Brower, "Mild Mannered Mel Fisher Defies the Deep to Recover a King's Ransom in Lost Treasure," *Illustrated People,* August 12, 1985, 63–70.

6. *Ibid.,* 70.

7. "Harlem Enterprise," *Success,* November 1986, 46–47.

8. Harold S. Kushner, *When All You've Ever Wanted Isn't Enough* (New York: Summit, 1986), 160.

9. Alan Jones, *Exploring Spiritual Direction: An Essay on Christian Friendship* (New York: Seabury Press, 1982), 42.

10. Peter Lyon, *Eisenhower: Portrait of a Hero* (Boston: Little, Brown, 1974), 82.

11. George Williams, "Emily Williams," *Notable American Women, 1607–1950: A Biographical Dictionary,* Vol. III, (Cambridge, Mass: Belknap Press, 1971), 22–23.

12. Connie Sherley, "Flores de Noche Buena," *Continental,* December 1986, 52.

13. Joseph P. Kahn, "Life after Success," *Inc.,* February 1986, 61–65.

14. William Shakespeare, *Julius Caesar,* IV, iii, 217, 222.

15. "Doug Wilder Carries Old Virginy, Making History As He Wins the Lieutenant Governorship," *Illustrated People,* December 9, 1985, 125–127.

16. "Harlem Enterprise," 46.

17. Luke 2:25–35.

## Chapter 4

1. William Shakespeare, *As You Like It,* II, vii, 139.

2. Maury Allen, *Jackie Robinson: A Life Remembered* (New York: Franklin Watts, 1987), 150.

3. *Ibid.*

4. Katherine Ames, "Beverly in Bloom," *Savvy,* May 1987, 33–35; 82–85.

5. "Scandal Stalls S.M.U.'s Climb to the Top," *Dallas Morning News,* April 12, 1987, 26A.

6. James A. Dubik, "An Officer and a Feminist," *Newsweek,* April 2, 1987, 7–8.

7. "Why Women Still Fail to Reach the Top," *Report on Business Magazine,* May 1985, 83.

8. "Hawaiian Dateline: Mrs. Fields Goes Nuts," *Western's World,* August 1986, 54–56.

9. "Introducing Bridgette Denevir: Pilot, Instructor and Aircraft Mechanic," *The Miami Herald,* December 19, 1986, 2B.

10. Doris Kearns Goodwin, "At JFK's Inauguration, Father's Dream Came True," *The Miami-Herald,* March 27, 1987, 2B.

11. *Ibid.*

12. Yvonne Duffy, "Revealing a Splendid Deception," *Kansas City Star,* June 30, 1987, D–7.; Hugh Gregory Gallager, *FDR's Splendid Deception* (New York: Dodd, Mead, 1987).

13. "Legless Marathoner Finishes on Arms, Grit," *Orlando Sentinel,* November 7, 1986, 1.

14. "Does Anyone Remember Who Came In First?", *Focus on the Family,* January 1987, 14.

15. "Jeff Keith's Incredible Run: A Proud Sponsor Moves In on Cancer," *National Relocation Magazine,* Spring 1986, 34.

16. Fucini and Fucini, 34–35.

17. *Ibid.,* 239.

18. Robert Sobel and David B. Sicila, "The Entrepreneur: An American Adventure," *Entrepreneur,* May 1987, 29.

19. Susan Sachs, "The New Generation of Entrepreneurs: Who Are They?" *Entrepreneur,* May 1987, 29.

20. Scully Blotnick, *Ambitious Men* (New York: Viking 1986), 106.

21. Mark 8:36–37.

22. Kushner, 146.

23. "Managing: Boone Speaks," *Fortune,* February 16, 1987, 56.

## Chapter 5

1. *USA Today,* May 22, 1987, 5F.
2. *USA Today,* May 22, 1987, 3F.
3. Walter S. Ross, *The Last Hero: Charles A. Lindbergh* (New York: Harper and Row, 1968), 79.
4. *Ibid.,* 80.
5. Charles A. Lindbergh, *The Spirit of St. Louis* (New York: Scribner's, 1933), 96–98, 152.
6. Ross, 98.
7. Lindbergh, 188; Ross, 110.
8. P. Ranganath Nayak and John M. Ketteringham, *Breakthroughs* (New York: Rawson Associates, 1986), 184–185.
9. "Vietnam Refugee Wins Wings after Padding His Posterior," *Atlanta Constitution,* June 20, 1987, 8–30.
10. Lindbergh, 34.
11. Lee Mars and Ross Y. Yosnow, "Funding Your Fantasy," *New Woman,* June 17, 1987, 107, 168.
12. *Ibid.*
13. Barbara Kallen, "If You're So Smart, Buy It Yourself," *Forbes,* May 18, 1987, 200.
14. Leviticus 26:8.
15. Fucini and Fucini, 29–32.
16. *Ibid.,* 209.
17. *Ibid.,* 229.
18. Personal interview, February 9, 1988, Nashville, Tennessee; "In the Chips," *Vanderbilt Magazine,* Spring 1987, 38.

## Chapter 6

1. Paul Tournier, *A Listening Ear: Reflections on Christian Caring,* trans. by Edwin Hudson (Minneapolis: Augsburg, 1987), 10, 33.
2. Martin Luther King, "I Have a Dream," in David J. Garrow, *Bearing the Cross: Martin Luther King, Jr.,* (New York: William Morrow, 1986), 283–284.
3. John Gunther, *The Riddle of MacArthur* (Westport, Conn.: Greenwood Press, 1974), 40.
4. Lerner, 226.
5. Lindbergh, 23.
6. Ross, 81–88.
7. Lindbergh, 30–32.
8. *Ibid.,* 34.
9. Tournier, 26.
10. Ross, 86.
11. *Ibid.*; Lindbergh, 86, 103.
12. Ross, 87.
13. *Ibid.,* 88.

14. "Surgeons Form Fingers for Boy," *Ft. Lauderdale Sun-Sentinel,* May 29, 1987, 2B.

15. Interview with Richard Greminger, May 29, 1987.

**Chapter 7**

1. Hebrews 11:1.
2. Hebrews 11:1 (J. B. Phillips).
3. Alan Jones, *Exploring Spiritual Direction: An Essay on Christian Friendship* (New York: Seabury Press, 1982), 42.
4. Genesis 1:1.
5. Genesis 1:2–3.
6. Hebrews 11:7, 8, 11, 24, 31.
7. Genesis 15:4 (NIV).
8. Genesis 15:5.
9. Genesis 18:13–14.
10. Hebrews 11:12 (NIV).
11. Lynne Duke, "Rev. Edward T. Graham, 82, Miami Civil Rights Leader," *The Miami-Herald,* March 30, 1987, 3B.
12. John Fooks, "A Long Struggle to Success," *Dallas Morning News,* December 15, 1985, 69A, 72A.
13. *Ibid.*
14. Ecclesiastes 9:11 (NIV).
15. Henry David Thoreau, *Walden,* "Conclusion," 18.
16. Lech Walensa, "Essay" in *The Courage of Conviction,* ed. by Phillip L. Berman (New York: Ballentine, 1985), 227.
17. *Ibid.*, 231.
18. *Ibid.*, 233.
19. Barbara Sher and Annie Gottlieb, *Wishcraft: How to Get What You Really Want out of Life* (New York: Ballentine, 1983), xiv.
20. Ida R. Bellegarde, *Black Heroes and Heroines* (Pine Bluff, Arkansas: Bell Enterprises, 1979), 37; see also *Notable American Women, 1607–1950, The Modern Period* (Cambridge: Belknap Press, 1980), 76–79.
21. Mary McLeod Bethune, *American Spiritual Autobiographies,* ed. by Louis Finkelstein (New York: Harper and Row, 1948), 189.
22. Florence Lovell Roane, "A Cultural History of Professional Teacher Education at Bethune-Cookman College," D.A. dissertation, Boston University, 1965; 89.
23. Leedell W. Neyland, *Twelve Black Floridians* (Tallahassee, Florida: Florida A & M Press, 1970), 20; Roane, 94.
24. "Woman of the Year: Cory Aquino," *Time,* January 5, 1987, 20; Phillip Yancey, "Prisons: Bulwarks Against Spiritual Bankruptcy," *Christianity Today* (32), February 5, 1988, 16; "Corazon Aquino," *1986 Current Biography Yearbook,* ed. by Charles Mortiz, (New York: Wilson, 1986), 17.
25. "Woman of the Year," *Time,* 20.

26. Sandra Burton, "Starting the Campaign with Hope and a Prayer," *Time,* January 5, 1987, 26.

27. "Woman of the Year," *Time,* 20.

28. Charles Colson with Ellen Santilli Vaughn, *Kingdoms in Conflict* (Grand Rapids: William Morrow/Zondervan, 1987), 323.

29. "A Christmas Conversation," *Time,* January 5, 1987, 33.

30. "Woman of the Year," *Time,* 27.

31. Colson and Vaughn, *Kingdoms in Conflict,* 327.

32. "Woman of the Year," *Time,* 27.

33. Hebrews 11:32.

34. Tim Stafford, *Knowing the Face of God* (Grand Rapids: Zondervan, 1986), 81–82.

35. Hebrews 12:1.

## Chapter 8

1. "Dreams Destroyed As Businesses Burn in Hayward," *San Francisco Chronicle,* January 12, 1987, Section 1, 7.

2. Newton, 16–17.

3. "The Navy Gets Ready to Bring Back the Blimp," *Business Week,* November 17, 1986, 159–160.

4. Mark Maremont, "Airship's Fortunes Are Suddenly Afloat," *Business Week,* June 22, 1987, 52.

5. Victor Frankl, *Man in Search of Meaning* (New York: Touchstone Books, 1984).

6. Psalm 137:4 (NIV).

7. Jeremiah 29:7.

8. Deuteronomy 4:29.

9. Daniel Boorstin, *The Americans: The National Experience* Vol. III (New York: Random, 1965), 431.

10. Genesis 28:13–15.

11. Genesis 28:16.

12. Lee Iacocca, *Iacocca: An Autobiography* (New York: Bantam, 1984), xv–xvi.

13. Romans 8:11.

14. Anthony Campolo, *Seven Deadly Sins* (Wheaton: Victor, 1986), 29.

15. Charles Converse, "What a Friend We Have in Jesus," *Worship in Song* (Kansas City: Lillenas, 1972), 123.

## Chapter 9

1. Newton, 19.

2. "New Arrests on Wall Street," *Newsweek,* February 23, 1987, 48; Ellen Goodman, "For Some People, There Is No 'Enough,'" *Kansas City Star,* February 23, 1987, A-7.

3. *Ibid.*

4. "Greed," *M Magazine,* October 1986, 105.

5. "Rebuilding to Survive," *Time,* February 16, 1987, 44–45.

6. Matthew 16:26.

7. Alfred Armand Montapert, *The Supreme Philosophy of Man,* rev. ed. (Los Angeles: Books of Value, 1970), 89.

8. Bill Norton, "The Many Lives of Del Dunmire," *Star Magazine,* March 1, 1987, 12–16.

9. *Ibid.*

10. Michael Walsh, "What Price Glory, Leontyne!" *Time,* January 14, 1985, 67.

11. "A Modest Bridge Party," *Time,* November 25, 1986, 31; John Van Der Zee, *The Gate: The True Story of the Design and Construction of the Golden Gate Bridge* (New York: Simon and Schuster, 1986), 123.

12. Evert Clark, "Now the Father of the Laser Can Get Back to Inventing," *Business Week,* February 17, 1986, 98.

13. Kushner, 1.

14. Paul Galloway, "Ambitious Men: How Four Seek to Climb Out of the Snakepit," *Chicago Tribune,* February 17, 1987, Section 5, 15.

15. "In America, Fame Is an Open Door," *U.S. News and World Report,* October 6, 1986, 65; see also, Leo Braudy *The Frenzy of Renown: Fame and Its History* (New York: Oxford University Press, 1986).

16. Galloway, 15.

17. *Ibid.*

18. Kahn, 65.

19. Clark, 98.

20. Ralph Waldo Emerson as quoted by Jim Tunney, in "Six Hour Seminar in Thirty Minutes," Tape: Voice of Experience, National Speakers Association, 1985.

21. Kushner, 161–162.

22. Gordon MacDonald, *Restoring Your Spiritual Passion* (Nashville: Oliver/Nelson, 1986), 165.

23. Norton, 33.

**Chapter 10**

1. William J. Bennett, "First Lessons," *Phi Delta Kappa,* October 1986, 125–126; see also, Christine S. Sleeter and Carl A. Grant, "Success for All Students," *Phi Delta Kappa,* December 1986, 297.

2. Harold Ivan Smith, "Teen Age Sexuality," *Ministry Today,* April–May 1987, 32–33.

3. James J. Kirkpatrick, "Lessons from the Japanese," *Kansas City Times,* January 9, 1987, A–11; and "American Youth Never Had It So Tough As Teen-agers of Japan," *Kansas City Times,* January 16, 1987, A–13.

4. Cathy M. Jackson, "Late Astronaut's Father Helps Pupils Learn from His Example," *Tampa Tribune,* January 26, 1988, PT–1, PT–2.

5. *Ibid.*

6. Samuel G. Sava, "Good Questions," *Phi Delta Kappa,* October 1986, 130.

7. Harold Hodgkinson quoted in Bennett, 126; William V. Shannon, "Unprecedented Demands on Schools," *Kansas City Times,* January 9, 1987, A–10.

8. "Perot at the Roundtable," remarks delivered at the Peabody College Roundtable, Vanderbilt University, October 10, 1985, reported in *Peabody Reflector,* Spring 1986, 27.

9. *Ibid.*

10. *Ibid.*

11. "Japanese Can Teach Much," *Miami-Herald,* December 21, 1986, Section 4, 7.

12. Perot, 27.

13. "A Capital Gift," *Success,* January/February 1987, 48.

14. Julia Taylor, "You Must Have a Dream," *USA Today,* December 24, 1987, 1A–2A.

15. Editorial: "Squeeze on Campus," *Los Angeles Times,* January 12, 1987, Section II, 4.

16. "Student Aid Tops 16 Million," *Vandy Today,* February 1986, 6.

17. Sava, 130.

18. *Time,* October 13, 1980, 19.

19. Maya Pines, "Superkids," *Psychology Today,* January 1979, 53.

20. *Ibid.*

21. Susan Littwin, *The Postponed Generation: Why American Youth Are Growing Up Later* (New York: William Morrow, 1986), 134.

22. *Ibid.*, 79.

23. *Ibid.*

24. Perot at Roundtable, 27.

25. Littwin, 37.

26. Kirkpatrick, "Lessons from the Japanese," A–11.

27. Bennett, 126.

28. "A Blueprint for Better Schools," *U.S. News & World Report,* January 18, 1988, 62–63.

29. *Ibid.*, 64.

30. *Ibid.*

31. Jules Olitski, Essay in *The Courage of Conviction,* ed. by Phillip L. Berman (New York: Ballentine, 1985), 188, 183.

## Chapter 11

1. Ad, "Many Champions Are Born and Then Unmade," Converse Corporation.

2. John Pollock, *Billy Graham: The Authorized Biography* (New York: McGraw-Hill, 1966), 52.

3. *Ibid.*, 53–54.

4. Genesis 37:4.

5. Genesis 37:20.

6. Joy E. Parnaby, "Sir Charles Givan Duffy," *Australian Dictionary of Biography, Volume 4: 1851–1890, D-J,* ed. by Bede Nairn (Melbourne: Melbourne University Press, 1986), 110.

7. Robert Hughes, *The Fatal Shore* (New York: Knopf, 1987), 181, 589–590; Marjorie Barnard, *A History of Australia* (New York: Fred Praeger, 1966), 452; Parnaby, 110–112; Joseph Kinsey Howard, *Montana: High, Wide and Handsome* (New York: Yale, 1959), 43–45; Clark C. Spence, *Montana: A Bicentennial History* (New York: Norton, 1978), 49–50.

8. Jim and Barb Dycus, *Not Guilty! From Convict to Christian* (San Francisco: Harper and Row, 1988).

9. Genesis 39:23.

10. Ron Grossman, "Shtetl Novelist Honed His Pen under the Gun," *Chicago Tribune,* October 20, 1986, Section 2, 3; "Call It Sleep," *Time,* February 22, 1988, 85–86.

11. Genesis 40:14.

12. Tony Mauro, "Hoover FBI File Followed Justice Stewart," *USA Today,* April 20, 1987, 5A.

13. Genesis 41:33.

14. Genesis 41:40.

15. Richard Shickel, *The Disney Version* (New York: Simon and Schuster, 1968), 303–307, 308.

16. *Ibid.*, 306.

17. Mei-Mei Chan, "'Red October' Author Scores a Direct Hit," *USA Today,* December 23, 1985, 1D–2D.

18. Genesis 45:4–5.

19. Genesis 45:15.

20. Genesis 41:51.

21. Genesis 41:52.

22. Ralph De Toledano, *RFK: The Man Who Would Be President* (New York: Putnam, 1987), 341.

23. "Bethune," in Finkelstein, 189.

24. *Ibid.*

25. Steven Allen, "Essay," in *The Courage of Conviction,* ed. by Phillip L. Berman (New York: Ballentine, 1985), 10–11.